MUMPSIMUS REVISITED

MUMPSIMUS REVISITED

Essays on Risk Management

H. FELIX KLOMAN

Published by Seawrack Press, Inc., 61 Ely's Ferry Road, Lyme, Connecticut 06371-3408, USA

CONTENTS

Dedication

To two writers in their own right, my daughter Blair, who corrected and trimmed the final text, and my wife Ann, who has been my loyal and critical copy editor since 1994.

FOREWORD

I like to write. I like to see my words in print, and I like to know that others read and may be affected by them. This book is a selection of essays on uncertainty, risk, and how we as individuals and as members of organizations and societies can begin to make better decisions when facing the probability that the outcomes will be unexpected. Most have appeared at some point in *Risk Management Reports,* a publication that I've written and edited since 1974.

First, what accounts for my fascination with writing? It began, I suspect, in the sixth grade in Philadelphia, when I persuaded my teacher to allow me to write a class newspaper. It was a bi-weekly, two-page publication and I was the reporter, editor, printer and distributor all rolled into one. I collected the information, interviewed both teachers and classmates, typed my material on a purple form and, every other Sunday in my father's church office, ran off copies on his mimeograph machine. I recall that my fascination lasted from late fall to early spring, when the baseball season intervened.

At boarding school in New Hampshire, I spent four years writing for the school's bi-weekly, *The Pelican,* becoming the Managing Editor by my Sixth Form year. A year later, at Princeton University, I spent the fall working for the *Daily Princetonian,* only to run headlong into the wall of time and sports again. I retreated to my course papers, ice hockey and the sailing team. I also retreated to writing, my senior year, a 207-page thesis on *The Culture of Colonial Newport,* into which I tried to cram every bit of research of a full year. I learned from that mistake: length does not equal quality!

The lure of writing did not subside, however, and after joining an insurance brokerage firm in Philadelphia, I wrote several articles that were published in the trade press. Then, while enrolled in a graduate seminar on international relations at the University of Pennsylvania, my professor suggested one day that I submit a paper to *The U. S. Naval Institute Proceedings* for publication. Not only was it accepted, but the *Proceedings* also paid me a handsome stipend of $50. That's when I learned that I could earn money from writing.

Seven years later, in New York, Rance Crain, of the family that owns Crain Communications, asked me to write some book reviews pertinent to risk management. I did, at first under the pseudonym *John Street,* as my employer felt that books such as Galbraith's *The New Industrial State,* Antony Jay's *Management and Machiavelli,* and the American Management Association's *Mobilizing for Urban Action—Challenge to Business* were "too controversial" to allow my name and the firm's to be seen in public!

By late 1969 I escaped both New York and the insurance business to start a new risk management consultancy in Connecticut. Almost immediately I planned a new publication, for which I would be editor and principal writer, one that we would sell on a subscription basis. In 1973, I suggested this new publication to Rance Crain and he agreed to become its publisher and distributor. The first issue of *Risk Management Reports (RMR)* rolled off the presses in January 1974. It started as a monograph of 20 to 40 pages on a single risk management subject, preceded by my "Current Comment," a personal perspective on events, people, articles, and books of interest. I promised "in-depth analyses of risk and insurance management subjects for the practical, everyday guidance of risk managers, insurance managers, and financial officers of corporations, financial institutions, and educational and governmental bodies." The goal: try and "bridge the gap between the theoretical and the practical." Three years later my firm took over the publishing responsibilities from Crain Communications, and I've continued as Editor ever since.

Through the 70s the publication covered product safety, annual reports, EDP security, risk retention levels, workers' compensation, social responsibility, the hold harmless clause, cost allocations, investment income, emergency planning, and insurance bidding and specifications— all highly practical.

In the 80s, I deliberately moved farther afield, trying to stretch the thinking of subscribers. Issues included information systems surveys, risk analysis in public policy, managing uncertainty, the confluence of banking and insurance, European and Asian views of risk management, the risk management audit, managing service providers, crisis management, political risks, multi-line aggregate programs, risk communication, alternative dispute resolution, and global risk management strategies.

In August 1993, I retired from Towers Perrin, the successor firm to my original consultancy. My partners and I could find no ready takers for the task of writing and editing *RMR,* so we decided to continue it as a monthly six-page publication, with my "personal observations on the fascinating and evolving world of risk management." It echoed my belief in a more holistic, integrated and strategic form of the discipline—a new approach to living with the uncertainties of modern living. I challenged the prevailing idea that risk involves only harm, arguing that reward is an equally important element in any diagnosis. In March 1994, Seawrack Press, Inc., a company that I formed on retirement, took over ownership. In April 2001, I shifted it from print to electronic distribution, its current mode.

What follows, as *Mumpsimus Revisited,* is a collection of *RMR* essays written over the last 15 years. How did I select the title of *Mumpsimus Revisited?* For that you'll have to read Chapter 1. Suffice it to say that my thoughts about risk management have changed and evolved as radically as the discipline. I have not been a model of consistency! Yet the twin faces of risk are now accepted (I saw only one in my early years). Risk is now a strategic challenge, not a tactical one, and its management requires balance. While we should address all risks strategically, we should take advantage of different tactical solutions, such as derivatives, swaps, hedges, options, insurance, credit, claims management, and public regulations. We are now far more sophisticated in our analyses of risk.

I also plead guilty to some repetition in the following essays, and especially in many of my favorite quotations from others. This propensity is attributable to my father, an Episcopal minister, who warned me that those you address won't learn unless you hit them several times. He recounted the famous story about the preacher who was asked about the success of his sermons. It was, he said, because "I tell them what I'm going to say; then I say it; and then I tell them what I just said." So please accept my repetition.

My continued goal is to listen and speak to everyone. We are all part of the same dynamic movement. I want to stretch my readers' minds beyond the constraints of their normal stimuli. As Roger Rosenblatt put it, "If we only learn what we believe we need to know, how will we discover those things we do not know that we need to know, or that we forget we need to know?" ("Ah, Cyberspace!" *Ideas*, Vol. 5, No. 1)

CHAPTER 1

Mumpsimus

Mumpsimus
(October 1995)

Am I guilty of the sin of mumpsimus?

In the early 1970s, I became enthusiastic about the idea of "cost-of-risk," as developed by Canada's Douglas Barlow, and spearheaded an effort to collect and publish cost-of-risk data from U.S. corporations (insurance premiums, uninsured losses, loss control costs and administrative expenses). I thought that they might provide a stimulus for risk management as something more than insurance—and also as benchmarks among similar organizations. We first published the data every two years and then moved to annual reports. During these years David Warren, the editor of *The Warren Report,* was a consistent and vocal critic, not of keeping cost-of-risk numbers but of attempting to use them as comparative bases for benchmarking. I first suggested that he might be "tilting at windmills" in his effort to derail cost-of-risk calculations and surveys. I argued that it might be better to try and refine the numbers and collection methodology, while avoiding misuse of the data.

I see, however, that I may have fallen into the trap of "mumpsimus" which, as a student of the English language knows, is the "adherence to or persistence in an erroneous use of language, practice or belief, *out of habit or obstinacy."*

The story goes that a medieval monk, in England or The Netherlands, had been using the phrase *"quod in ore mumpsimus"* when reading the Eucharist, when the word should have been *"sumpsimus"* (meaning "we have taken"). When challenged the monk claimed he'd been reading it that way for forty years and had no intention of changing his habit.

My enthusiasm for the idea of cost-of-risk and my long association with the development of the survey made me obstinate. I underestimated the real statistical limitations that David Warren noted: the variability of respondents from one year to the next, the lack of definition in the numbers, the variability of insurance limits and deductibles, and the range of possible costs. David Warren noted that too many of us are functionally innumerate, despite dealing with numbers every day. It was David who led me to read a remarkable book by John Allen Paulos, entitled *Innumeracy: Mathematical Illiteracy and its Consequences.*

Two of Paulos's comments are pertinent. (1) "Even more ominous is the gap between scientists' assessments of various risks and the popular perceptions of those risks, a gap that threatens eventually to lead either to unfounded and crippling anxieties or to impossible and economically paralyzing demands for risk-free guarantees." And (2) "... innumerate people characteristically have a strong tendency to personalize—to be misled by their own experiences or by the media's focus on individuals and drama."

This leaves us with cost-of-risk primarily as an internal measure of change from one year to the next. I still believe that, with carefully spelled out definitions, internal cost-of-risk calculations are useful tools for senior management. Having said this, I now find that what we need is an *overall* measure of the "cost" (present and future) of taking *all* forms of risk: operational, political/regulatory, credit, market and reputation. The original and current construction of the cost-of-risk survey is inadequate for this purpose.

I suspect that we will develop new econometric models of organizational risk. Risk changes almost daily, and we need a methodology to measure in a continuous fashion risk against equity (if a profit-making organization), budget (if a governmental organization), or assets (if a nonprofit). RAROC, VaR and other measures begin to provide useful guidance.

The key questions become: what is the total current "value" or "cost" of *all* forms of risk affecting an organization, and what should we be doing about these risks? The idea of cost-of-risk must move on.

I am renouncing my mumpsimus. We need a new measurement tool.
I changed my mind in 1995 after 20 years of supporting one idea.
Here is one in which I have not changed my mind (yet).

New Challenge for Risk Management
(May-June 1977)

President Carter's call for conservation as the keystone of the nation's energy policy is both realistic and responsible. Faced with an insatiable demand for limited energy resources, we can respond by beginning to make major adjustments to our style of living. New energy sources, such as fusion and solar, are possible, but for the near term we, and the remainder of the developed world, will continue to depend on fossil fuels. Of course, we could feed our appetites through an unrestricted search for new fossil fuel sources, such as strip mining and offshore drilling, but the combination of the chance of ecological damage and the high cost to undertake this work makes this alternative both unworkable and unthinkable. Conservation is and must be the prime response.

The corporate risk manager has a new challenge as we respond to this call for conservation. If, as I believe, the risk manager's role is, in its largest sense, the conservation of all corporate resources—human, physical, natural and financial—from risks of loss or waste, then I hope that at least some risk managers in the United States will forge new programs for conservation. It's easy to say that conservation is the job of the CEO, or someone else, and that *my* job is just insurance. *Someone,* however, will take this new responsibility and *someone* will develop the internal program to respond to social, legal and technological pressures. That *someone* can and should be a person with a broad overview of corporate activities, knowledge of the financial facts of life, and established personal relationships with both senior and operating managers. An effective risk manager may have the requisite position, education and experience for this job.

CHAPTER 2

A Brief History of Risk Management

The process of making good decisions in the face of uncertainty and risk began at the earliest point of human existence. Experience and new information allowed us to think intelligently about the future and plan for potential unexpected outcomes. While many millennia contributed to our growing ability to distill and use information, the developments of the 20th century are more apparent and useful to us. What follows is synopsis of critical events over the past one hundred years.

Milestones: 1900 to 1999
(December 1999)

As a child, I was fascinated by the puzzle with a page full of numbered dots which, when connected, revealed a picture. As this millennium ends (actually we have another year to go, but that's not how we plan to celebrate), I created a picture of the risk management discipline by describing and connecting some of its milestones. It is a personal list. I'm sure that readers could add other important dates and events, but I hope that linking them will give us a better understanding of the discipline.

The 20th century started with euphoria, new wealth, relative peace and industrialization, only to descend into chaos, a series of regional and worldwide wars. These and other catastrophes crushed illusions about the perfectibility of society and our species, leaving us less idealistic and more appreciative of the continuing uncertainty of our future.

Ideas drove change in this century. Stephen Lagerfeld summed it up cogently in his "Editor's Comment" in the Autumn 1999 issue of *Wilson*

Quarterly: "Apart from the almost accidental tragedy of World War I, the great clashings of our bloody century have not been provoked by the hunger for land, or riches, or other traditional sources of national desire, but by *ideas*—about the value of individual dignity and freedom, about the proper organization of society, and ultimately about the possibility of human perfection."

Risk management is one of those ideas—the sense that a logical, consistent and disciplined approach to the future's uncertainties will allow us to live with them prudently and productively, avoiding unnecessary waste of resources. It goes beyond faith and luck, the twin pillars of managing the future before we began learning how to measure probability. As Peter Bernstein wrote, in *Against the Gods: The Remarkable Story of Risk,* "If everything is a matter of luck, risk management is a meaningless exercise. Invoking luck obscures truth, because it separates an event from its cause."

If risk management is an extension of human nature, I could arguably list as critical most of the notable political, economic, military, scientific and technological events of the past 100 years. The major wars, from the Russo-Japanese, World Wars I and II, and Korea, to the regional conflicts that have followed, the advent of the automobile, radio, television and the computer, the Great Depression, global warming, the atom bomb and nuclear power, the rise and fall of communism, derivatives fiascoes, and the entire environmental movement have affected the development of risk management. Major catastrophes did so more directly: the Titanic, the Triangle Shirtwaist fire, Minimata Bay, Seveso, Bhopal, Chernobyl, Three Mile Island, Challenger, Piper Alpha and Exxon Valdez, to cite some of the more obvious. Earthquakes, tsunamis, typhoons, cyclones and hurricanes continue to devastate populous regions, and their increasing frequency and severity stimulate new studies on causes, effects, and prediction, all part of the evolution of risk management.

Yet the most significant milestones, at least in my opinion, are more personal: the new ideas, books, and actions of *individuals* who stimulated the discipline. Here's my list:

1905-1912 The advent of workers' compensation laws in the United States, based on their introduction in Germany in 1881 by Chancellor

Otto von Bismarck. These "social insurance" schemes proliferated worldwide, leading also to government provision of pensions (social security) in most countries in the 1930s and afterwards. They signaled a shift from individual responsibility to corporate and governmental.

1920   The formation of Tanker Insurance Company, Ltd., one of the first captive insurance companies, beginning a movement that exploded in the 1970s and 1980s. Today there are over 4,100 such companies worldwide, counting $21.3 billion in annual premiums. Captives illustrate the idea of prudent internal financing of risk, as compared to trying to shift it outside the organization.

1921   Frank Knight publishes *Risk, Uncertainty and Profit*, a book that becomes the keystone in the risk management library. Knight separates uncertainty, which is not measurable, from risk, which is. He celebrates the prevalence of "surprise" and he cautions against over-reliance on extrapolating past frequencies into the future.

1921   *A Treatise on Probability,* by John Maynard Keynes, appears. He too scorns dependence on the "Law of Great Numbers," emphasizing the importance of relative perception and judgment when determining probabilities.

1926   John von Neumann presents his first paper on a theory of games and strategy at the University of Göttingen, suggesting that the goal of not losing is superior to that of winning. Later, in 1953, he and Oskar Morgenstern publish *The Theory of Games and Economic Behavior.*

1933   The U.S. Congress passes the Glass-Steagall Act, prohibiting common ownership of banks, investment banks and insurance companies. This Act, finally revoked in late 1999, arguably acted as a brake on the development of financial institutions in the United States and led the risk management discipline in many ways to be more fragmented than integrated. The unnecessary split between financial and insurance risks continues to this day.

1945   Congress passes the McCarran-Ferguson Act, delegating the regulation of insurance to the various states, rather than to the

Federal government, even as business became more national and international. This put another needless brake on risk management, as it hamstrung the ability of the insurance industry to become more responsive to the broader risks of its commercial customers.

1952 The *Journal of Finance* publishes "Portfolio Selection," by Dr. Harry Markowitz, who later wins the Nobel Prize in 1990. It explores aspects of return and variance in an investment portfolio, leading to many of the sophisticated measures of financial risk in use today.

1956 *Harvard Business Review* publishes "Risk Management: A New Phase of Cost Control," by Russell Gallagher, then the insurance manager of Philco Corporation in Philadelphia. This city is the focal point for new "risk management" thinking, from Dr. Wayne Snider, then of the University of Pennsylvania, who suggested that "the professional insurance manager should be a risk manager," (*National Underwriter*, November 1955) to Dr. Herbert Denenberg, another Penn professor who began exploring the idea of risk management using some early writings of Henri Fayol.

1962 In Toronto, Douglas Barlow, the insurance risk manager at Massey Ferguson, develops the idea of "cost-of-risk," comparing the sum of self-funded losses, insurance premiums, loss control costs, and administrative costs to revenues, assets and equity. This moves insurance risk management thinking away from insurance, but it still fails to cover all forms of financial and political risk.

That same year Rachel Carson's *The Silent Spring* challenges the public to consider seriously the degradation to our air, water and ground from both inadvertent and deliberate pollution. Her work leads directly to the creation of the Environmental Protection Agency in the United States in 1970, the plethora of today's environmental regulations, and the global Green movement so active today.

1965 The Corvair unmasked! Ralph Nader's *Unsafe at Any Speed* appears and gives birth to the consumer movement, first in the United States and later moving throughout the world, in which *caveat vendor* replaces the old precept of *caveat emptor*. The ensuing wave of litigation and regulation leads to stiffer product, occupational safety, and security regulations in most developed nations. Public outrage at corporate misbehavior also leads to the rise of punitive damages in American courts.

1966   The Insurance Institute of America develops a set of three examinations that lead to the designation "Associate in Risk Management," the first such certification. While heavily oriented toward corporate insurance management, its texts feature a broader risk management concept and are revised continuously, keeping the ARM curriculum up-to-date.

1972   Dr. Kenneth Arrow wins the Nobel Memorial Prize in Economic Science, along with Sir John Hicks. Arrow imagines a perfect world in which every uncertainty is "insurable," a world in which the Law of Large Numbers works without fail. He then points out that our knowledge is always incomplete—it "comes trailing clouds of vagueness"—and that we are best prepared for risk by accepting its potential as both a stimulant and a penalty.

1973   In 1971, a group of insurance company executives meet in Paris to create the International Association for the Study of Insurance Economics. Two years later, The Geneva Association, its more familiar name, holds its first Constitutive Assembly and begins linking risk management, insurance and economics. Under its first Secretary General and Director, Orio Giarini, the Geneva Association provides intellectual stimulus for the developing discipline.

That same year, Myron Scholes and Fischer Black publish their paper on option valuation in the *Journal of Political Economy* and we begin to learn about derivatives.

1974   Gustav Hamilton, the risk manager for Sweden's Statsforetag, creates a "risk management circle," graphically describing the interaction of all elements of the process, from assessment and control to financing and communication.

1975   In the United States, the American Society of Insurance Management changes its name to the Risk & Insurance Management Society (RIMS), acknowledging the shift toward risk management first suggested by Gallagher, Snider and Denenberg in Philadelphia twenty years earlier. By the end of the century, RIMS has 3,500 corporate members, some 7,000 deputy members, and a wide range of educational programs and services aimed primarily at insurance risk managers in North America. It links with sister associations in many other countries around the world through IFRIMA, the International Federation of Risk & Insurance Management Associations.

1976 With RIMS support, *Fortune* magazine publishes an article of mine, entitled "The Risk Management Revolution." It suggests the coordination of formerly unconnected risk management functions within an organization and acceptance by the board of responsibility for preparing an organizational policy and oversight of the function. Twenty years lapse before many of the ideas in this paper gain general acceptance.

1979 Daniel Kahneman and Amos Tversky publish their "prospect theory," demonstrating that human nature can be perversely irrational, especially in the face of risk, and that the fear of loss often trumps the hope of gain.

1980 Public policy, academic and environmental risk management advocates form the Society for Risk Analysis (SRA) in Washington. *Risk Analysis,* its quarterly journal, appears the same year. By 1999, SRA has over 2,200 members worldwide and active sub-groups in Europe and Japan. Through its efforts, the terms "risk assessment" and "risk management" are familiar in North American and European legislatures.

1983 William Ruckelshaus delivers his speech on "Science, Risk and Public Policy" to the National Academy of Sciences, launching the risk management idea in public policy. Ruckelshaus had been the first director of the Environmental Protection Agency, from 1970-73, and returned in 1983 to lead the EPA into a more principled framework for environmental policy. Risk management reaches the national political agenda.

1986 The Institute for Risk Management begins in London. Several years later, under the guidance of Dr. Gordon Dickson, it begins an international set of examinations leading to the designation, "Fellow of the Institute of Risk Management," the first continuing education program looking at risk management in all its facets.

That same year the U.S. Congress passes a revision to the Risk Retention Act of 1982, substantially broadening its application, in light of an insurance cost and availability crisis. By 1999, some 73 "risk retention groups"—effectively captive insurance companies under a federal mandate—account for close to $750 million in premiums.

1987   "Black Monday," October 19, 1987, hits the U.S. stock market. Its shockwaves are global, reminding all investors of the inherent risk and volatility in the market.

That same year Dr. Vernon Grose, a physicist, student of systems methodology, and former member of the National Transportation Safety Board, publishes *Managing Risk: Systematic Loss Prevention for Executives,* a book that remains one of the best, and clearest, primers on risk assessment and management.

1990   The United Nations Secretariat authorizes the start of IDNDR, the International Decade for Natural Disaster Reduction, a ten-year effort to study the nature and effects of natural disasters, particularly on the less-developed areas of the world, and to build a global mitigation effort. IDNDR concludes in 1999 but is continued by ISDR, the International Strategy for Disaster Reduction. Much of its work is detailed in *Natural Disaster Management,* a 319 page synopsis on the nature of hazards, social and community vulnerability, risk assessment, forecasting, emergency management, prevention, science, communication, politics, financial investment, partnerships, and the challenge for the 21st century.

1992   The Cadbury Committee issues its report in the United Kingdom, suggesting that governing boards are responsible for setting risk management policy, assuring that the organization understands all its risks, and accepting oversight for the entire process. Its successor committees (Hempel and Turnbull), and similar work in Canada, the United States, South Africa, Germany and France, establish a new and broader mandate for organizational risk management.

Also that year, British Petroleum (BP) turns conventional insurance risk financing topsy-turvy with its decision, based on an academic study by Neil Doherty of the University of Pennsylvania and Clifford Smith of the University of Rochester, to dispense with any commercial insurance on its operations in excess of $10 million. Other large, diversified, transnational corporations immediately study the BP approach.

The Bank for International Settlements issues its Basel I accord to help financial institutions measure their credit and market risks and set capital accordingly.

1993 The title "Chief Risk Officer" is first used by James Lam, at GE Capital, to describe a function to manage "all aspects of risk," including risk management, back-office operations, and business and financial planning. Today, based on James Lam's research, there are "over 50 CROs," responsible for multiple risk functions.

1995 A multi-disciplinary task force of Standards Australia and Standards New Zealand publishes the first *Risk Management Standard,* AS/NZS 4360:1995 (since revised in 1999 and 2004), bringing together for the first time several of the different sub-disciplines. This standard is followed by similar efforts in Canada, Japan and United Kingdom. While some observers think the effort premature, because of the constantly evolving nature of risk management, most hail it as an important first step toward a common global frame of reference.

That same year Nick Leeson, in Singapore, finds himself disastrously over-extended and manages to topple Barings. This unfortunate event, a combination of greed, hubris, and inexcusable control failures, receives world headlines and becomes the "poster child" for fresh interest in operational risk management.

1996 The Global Association of Risk Professionals, representing credit, currency, interest rate, and investment risk managers, starts in New York and London. An organization attuned to the new Internet world, it operates electronically, without official offices or staff. By 1999, it has over 8,000 members.

That same year, risk and risk management make the best seller lists in North America and Europe with the publication of Peter

Bernstein's *Against the Gods: The Remarkable Story of Risk*. Now in paperback and translated into eleven different languages, this single book, more than any of the preceding papers, speeches, books, ideas, or governmental acts, popularizes our understanding of risk and our attempts to manage it.

Perhaps Bernstein's book is the fitting end to this list of 20th century risk management milestones, since it illustrates the importance of communication. Too often, new ideas have been unnecessarily restricted to the cognoscenti. Arcane mathematics, academic prose and the secretiveness of various risk management "guilds" anxious to keep intruders out, leave many of us out of the process of contributing to this new discipline. Bernstein's lucid prose, compelling syntheses of difficult concepts, and personal portraits of those with new ideas, bring us an appreciation of the benefits that risk management can bestow on both organizations and individuals. Communication of what we learn about risk, both positive and negative, is the next hurdle.

And yet none of this looking backward will have any meaning or value unless it also acts as a stimulant for looking forward more prudently, intelligently, and optimistically, using the ideas and tools that the past century has given us. So let's step out and create some new risk milestones.

CHAPTER 3

Risk Management (1975-1999)

Over the years, I've written numerous pieces on the discipline of risk management. Here are several, beginning with 1975, running through 1999. Chapter 4 includes my more recent views.

A Thought on Risk Management
(May 1975)

In risk management, we are more often than not forced to deal with the end results—losses—of our exposure to risk, because of our incapability of correctly anticipating and controlling potential loss situations. In fact, a major industry—insurance—has developed over some two hundred years to deal with these after-the-loss situations.

This is called "half-way technology." An after-the-fact effort is made to correct our inability to prevent loss. Better is a "decisive technology," one that deals in anticipation and control. Its objective is the elimination of waste and the conservation of resources. Its key is the understanding of the elements of risk and the nature of exposures to loss, and recognition that the price of prevention is *never* as high as the cost of a "half-way technology."

While a "half-way technology" exists of necessity today it hardly means that we can rest, using the enormous industry it has spawned as a crutch.

In fact, if we are successful in our efforts to create a "decisive technology," one that is capable of anticipating and controlling loss events, then we should be able to dismantle large segments of the insurance industry.

Risk management remains an incomplete technology itself, but it is growing slowly and decisively through the addition of small pieces of practical experience and theoretical knowledge provided by those working in the area.

A Load of Breezes
(October 1997)

> How hot the pedlar, panting with his pack
> Of fans—a load of breezes on his back!
>
> **Kako, in** *A Net of Fireflies,* **translated by Harold Stewart (Charles E. Tuttle Co. 1960)**

Contradictions and ironies confuse and delight our modern world just as they did the Japanese poet over a century ago. Can today's corporation, laden with the uncertainties of the global economy, find relief within these risks themselves? This is the question facing strategic risk management.

Instead of looking at risk negatively—as a chance that some future event may cause harm—some organizations now recognize that risk includes inherent opportunity. Future success depends on both taking advantage of the benefits and reducing the harms from risk. The relationship between gain and loss depends on how well the risk is managed. An example: I traveled from London to Paris several months ago on the Eurostar. An electrical failure stopped us at the mouth of the Chunnel, delaying our arrival in Paris by 45 minutes. Not only did the train operators keep the passengers fully informed about the delay, but they also offered a free one-way ticket to compensate for the inconvenience. Here is a perfect example of transforming misfortune into opportunity. The railroad took advantage of the "fans" on its back and created goodwill when it first appeared to have lost it.

Too often today, risks remain contained and managed within separate compartments. A financial officer manages currency hedges and interest rate swaps. Credit managers review supplier and customer balance sheets. Legal staffers supervise political risks and regulatory compliance.

Engineers oversee environmental, safety, and health issues for personnel and neighbors. Insurance managers organize operational and legal liability risk financing. These specialists sit in their isolated castles, use arcane skills and jargon, and generally miss opportunities and inter-relationships as they over-focus on potential negative outcomes. Risks remain discrete, but most are connected and present numerous inherent opportunities. They must be viewed in a more holistic fashion.

This view demands new risk assessment tools. Such tools will define risk correlations and inter-dependencies so that organizational responses are more strategic and efficient. While financial/market, regulatory/political, legal liability and operational risks may require separate specialists for tactical day-to-day management, someone must provide a strategic overview of both opportunities and harm. Someone must "balance risk," using the words of Bankers Trust's Charles Sanford. Strategic, or holistic, or integrated, risk management, becomes today's answer: the new way of dealing with uncertainty.

This new philosophy for management calls for a commensurate change in both the attitudes and the organizational structure of external risk management service providers. The problem is that too few have the vision to discard outmoded approaches and search for new solutions. Unfortunately, one service provider, the insurance industry, appears to be reacting more like a slug than a gazelle. It is rapidly diminishing in importance.

New communications tools are radically changing old relationships. Electronic transmission of information and global access to data mean that intermediaries may not be essential in the arrangement and purchase of insurance. Underwriting information moves electronically to underwriters, and quotations, policy wording and financial data flow back, quickly, accurately and without the intervention of insurance agents and brokers. Intermediaries are outmoded. Today's managers need seasoned advisors who are not connected to the financing transaction.

All forms of advisors to the risk management process will see their traditional turf disappear. Accountants, brokers, consultants, lawyers, and engineers are essentially purveyors of information. With the Internet and the World Wide Web as a resource, will these services and skills be required? One U.S. risk manager now creates special project teams drawing proven individuals from different outside organizations, rather than dealing with a single firm. The team is linked through a dedicated Internet group, increasing mutual communication and efficiency. The Internet today does what a corporate group did yesterday. It creates and manages a highly skilled network.

It's ironic to see the current rush to merge insurance broking houses into larger monoliths, still chained to the commission system, when clients are dispensing with their services and moving to smaller, more flexible, fee-based advisors, called upon only when required. New technology accommodates this approach.

Risk management is now a Board issue, as a result of the Cadbury Committee and Dey Committee recommendations in the United Kingdom and Canada, and the new Risk Management Standard in Australia and New Zealand. The new risk view is no longer local or regional, but global. *All* risks now come under the purview of senior management, even as specialists continue to direct their attention to their respective risks. Internal and external multi-disciplinary "teams" are created to deal with the most current risk situations, incorporating solutions within new, flexible contingency plans. Knowledge of risks and the organization's responses to them are communicated to all stakeholders, acknowledging their different interests: shareholders, employees, customers, suppliers, regulators, communities in which the organization operates, and the public. The risk management team, no longer subservient to finance, legal affairs or administration, acts as an independent staff function networking with other staff and line responsibilities.

Risk financing is also becoming more holistic and strategic. The new approach assumes that all risks are somehow fundable, using the total resources of the organization. This makes much less important the conventional insurance and reinsurance industry. Traditional underwriting calls for an actuarial base of losses, spread of risk, homogeneity, randomness and the operation of the law of large numbers. Yet when the insurance industry applies these rules, it finds itself competing to finance the same risks that most large corporations can easily self-fund. The industry may be relatively efficient in funding losses less than US$10 million, but interest, acumen, and financial security diminish rapidly for risks in excess of that figure. The insurance industry also saddles its policies with numerous exclusions and offers limits of protection that are often dwarfed by its customers' exposure requirements. When limits of over $2 billion plus are needed, the industry often offers only $100 million. Its global surplus is only 14% of the market capitalization of the world's 50 largest companies and less than 3% of the assets of the world's 50 largest banks. Is the industry slipping into financial insignificance when compared to the needs of its customers and other financial institutions?

The transformation of risk financing is the freshest "breeze." Over the past quarter century managers responsible for risk financing have steadily moved away from conventional insurance toward increased self-funding, internal reserves, captive insurers, pools and innovative use of credit and capital markets. They carry their own solutions on their backs. The insurance industry, somewhat pejoratively, calls this the "Alternative Market." In fact, it is now the "primary market." Insurance has become the "alternative." Recent analyses in the United States and Europe show that these "primary" mechanisms account for 30% to 40% of all risk financing, but these studies are limited to those risks defined as conventionally "insurable." Add to those numbers the financial/market, regulatory/ political, and public forms of risk financing, and it is easy to see that insurance plays a minor role—probably less than 10% of total organizational strategic risk financing.

The key idea behind new strategic risk financing is that *risk is shared, not transferred*. Unfortunately insurance has often given (and been sold as) the illusion that someone else has accepted the problem. No matter how completely we try to fund risk, hidden and intangible costs remain. Our risk remains our responsibility. The new form of risk financing recognizes this and constructs a program to protect not only the balance sheet, but also the reputation of the organization. Recovery of business interruption or physical damage insurance does little to save a company if its reputation is destroyed. This naturally leads to much higher retention levels, as managers recognize that internal funding is both less expensive (given the high overhead costs of insurance) and a greater stimulant to rigorous risk control. Risk financing relationships today are being built on composite arrangements incorporating internal funding, captives, pools, credit, capital markets and, where cost-effective, insurance. These plans require longer-term relationships, ranging from five to ten years, building on the idea of partnership over time rather than on the more volatile annual re-negotiation of protection. Long-term plans permit risk managers to devote more time to risk assessment, risk communication, and risk control, where the payoffs are larger.

One unresolved problem is catastrophe. When larger trans-national organizations face risks where losses could easily exceed US$2 billion, they find an insurance market too thinly capitalized and too fragmented to provide the high levels of protection needed. Risk managers want financial partners that can take, on a net basis, as much or more risk than they themselves accept. How many insurers or reinsurers today can take, net, up to and over US$100 million, a not-uncommon retention for larger corporations? As before, the possible solutions may be carried on their own backs. Greater post-loss "pooling" arrangements with other large organizations, supported in part by insurance and by local, regional, and global disaster funding, may provide the necessary solution and financial security. More private stimulation of public-private consortia for major catastrophes, man-made or natural, could resolve the problem.

The strategic risk management idea is born of the recognition that we carry on our own backs the solutions to our problems.

Of course, all of this may be simply one person's biased surmise! As another Japanese poet, Koyo, wrote:

> *Autumn night on the river, with a moon;*
> *My neighbor's flute is playing, out of tune!*

From Ithaca to Cold Mountain
(July 1998)

Some years ago, Robertson Davies, perhaps Canada's finest writer, noted that "all my life long, reading has been my great refuge and solace." He encouraged each of us to join what he called "the clerisy," those who read extensively and widely. Davies argued that literature is the expression of the human spirit through the ages and that it brings benefit to everything we do. I've been engulfed lately with books, articles and speeches about risk financing and risk management, and I may be sliding into a dangerously limited rut. We all slip easily into repetitive reading habits—the business press, trade publications, the counsel of professional "experts." As problems increase and time diminishes, we unconsciously narrow our perspectives. Roger Rosenblatt summarized this problem last year, in *Ideas* (Fall, 1997): "If we only learn what we believe we need to know, how will we discover those things we do not know that we need to know, or that we forget that we need to know."

My suggestion: follow Robertson Davies' example and carve out time to read more widely. Good literature will expand the senses and allow better management decisions. I offer some examples from the old and new: Homer's *Odyssey*, written more than 2,700 years ago, and Charles Frazier's 1997 prize-winning novel, *Cold Mountain*. Both are voyages of discovery, treks toward remembered homes, returns to destiny. In the first, only Odysseus survives; in *Cold Mountain*, W. P. Inman, the Confederate deserter, achieves his goal only to lose his life in a moment of charitable hesitation. It may be stretching interpretation, but I find four useful risk management lessons in these works, lessons that seldom show up in business writing.

- **Managing risk involves moral ambiguities:** Homer describes a vengeful Odysseus sacking a city, sacrificing his own crew and finally slaughtering his wife's suitors after his return to Ithaca. Inman, sickened by war and death, still resorts to killing on his return trip. Risks and their responses create the same ambiguities. A vaccine that saves tens of thousands will probably kill or injure a few. Nonsteroidal anti-inflammatory drugs relieve much pain and are used more than 150 million times a year, but they account for some 80,000 hospitalizations and 8000 deaths. The automobile airbag saves lives, but some die because of it. There are moral difficulties and compromises in every risk decision we take: we cannot avoid them.

- **Watch out for unintended consequences:** This is an extension of the first thought. Odysseus, on leaving the blinded Polyphemus, unwisely and boastfully announces his name, drawing on his crew the adverse winds of Poseidon, the Cyclops' father. Inman, in his moment of mercy, unwilling to finish off a wounded boy, is shot himself. Having assessed the likelihood and consequences of a possible event, we take action that itself creates new risks. Unfortunately, in the heady atmosphere of a decision, we seldom consider unintended consequences. Ford Motor Company carefully used the most current cost-benefit analyses in determining the location of a gas tank on the Pinto, saving millions of dollars and assuring jobs and sales. But in a lawsuit after the death of a passenger in a car fire, a jury found Ford's analysis too callous and cold-blooded. It awarded enormous punitive damages.

- **Prepare for contingencies but expect surprises:** Odysseus prepared for his journey armed with his noted wiles, a sound craft, a loyal crew and frequent prayers to the gods, but he was the only one to reach Ithaca ten years later. Inman armed himself with a pistol, loaded backpack and his tactics of evasion, only to relax his guard on reaching home, where he lost his life. All contingency plans are imperfect. Flexibility, resiliency and vigilance are the critical ingredients of any plan.

- **Life is exploration and adventure—don't avoid risk:** Both Odysseus and Inman ranged widely from their courses to help others and grasp opportunities, but each persisted in his fundamental goal. Avoiding risk is not an option. Progress requires exploration, adventure, adaptation and change.

Am I stretching these literary analogies? I don't think so. David Block, a medical doctor and perspicacious reader from Georgia, agrees with my thesis. He sees risk management in its "organic, integrative sense as an intrinsically moral action that is distinctively literary, even aesthetic. It seeks harmony, efficiency, equilibrium and a wholeness of approach." He argues that risk management is a "remarkably human approach to mortality and desire, two uniquely human conceptions (deceptions?)" and that "it is in literature that we humans extend our experience and, in so doing, make greater experiencing possible for ourselves and others." Reaching out beyond conventional boundaries, personal and literary, enables us to live with life's uncertainties more creatively.

David also quotes from C. S. Lewis (*An Experiment in Criticism,* Cambridge University Press, 1965): "Literary experience heals the wound, without undermining the privilege of individuality. There are mass emotions (that) heal the wound; but they destroy the privilege. In them our separate selves are pooled and we sink back into sub-individuality. But in reading great literature I become a thousand men and yet remain myself. Like the night sky in the Greek poem, I see with myriad eyes, but it is still I who sees. Here, as in worship, in love, in moral action, and in knowing, I transcend myself; and am never more myself than when I do."

So, as a starter, go and read *The Odyssey* again. Stretch your mind.

Strategies for the Future
(March 1999)

I recently finished reading Samuel Eliot Morison's *The Great Explorers,* a history of the fearless European discoverers of America. The Cabots, John and Sebastian, Verrazzano, Cartier, Frobisher, Davis, Columbus, Magellan and Drake all sought new worlds and new frontiers, risking their lives, and often losing them, for the rewards of discovery, riches, a passage to China, and the praise of royalty. Their incredible willingness to accept great risk provides a dramatic distinction to today's world, in which our self-satisfied society tries to avoid risk.

Morison's point was that taking risk is the greatest stimulant to societal progress. It is a point worth re-emphasizing. The key for the next decade, if not the next century, must be to relish, not evade, uncertainty. And here is where the discipline of intelligent risk management becomes important to our society and its organizations. Old methods of risk management are outmoded: new approaches are needed. Using the knowledge and tools at their disposal, the great explorers didn't avoid risk; they tried to balance it. That same point was echoed several years ago by Charles Sanford, when he was chairman of Bankers Trust: balancing risk enables us to reach new frontiers. The survival and the success of those who practice risk management depend on understanding this point.

How can risk managers contribute more effectively to their organizations in the next decade? What skills will be most useful? I suggest seven ideas, as follows:

1. **Educate Yourself.** Risk management is now multi-disciplinary. It involves public policy, finance, safety, security, contingency planning, psychology, quality assurance, and human relations, among other skills. The discovery of new worlds comes from listening to unfamiliar disciplines, those that also practice risk management. One of the serious failures of the past decade has been the inability or unwillingness of the major groups that represent the different forms of risk management to reach out to each other. Each seems to adopt a parochial interest in protecting its own turf. That restricts the relentless momentum toward integration of risk management. What are some of these groups? The Global Association of Risk Professionals (GARP) represents financial risk management practitioners. It is the newest and probably will be the largest within a year, having over 5000 members in 80 countries now. It is a virtual organization, existing on the Internet without offices or paid employees. The Society for Risk Analysis (SRA), formed in 1980, represents 2200 global public policy, environmental and academic risk managers. The International Federation of Risk & Insurance Management Associations (IFRIMA) includes insurance risk managers in many national associations, such as the 4500-corporate-member Risk & Insurance Management Society in North America, a group formed in 1949. Other organizations representing risk management practitioners include the American Society of Safety Engineers (ASSE) and related global groups, the public accounting profession (AICPA in the United States, CICA in Canada, ICAEW in United Kingdom and IIA globally), The International Emergency Management Society (TIEMS), security groups, and quality assurance associations. Interaction among these groups has been modest. In the coming decade, risk managers should actively join their counterparts. Invite them to your meetings. Go to theirs. Create your own discussion sessions. It's the only way we can reach the goal of integrated risk management.

2. **Communicate Clearly.** What do we mean by "risk," "risk management," and "risk financing?" Are these terms clear to everyone in the organization? Adopt clear and simple definitions that are globally accepted. The International Standards Organization (ISO) is circulating a draft set of such definitions in English, as English is now the global language of business, economics, technology and politics. Ironically, I find that those who speak and write English as a second language often do it with greater clarity than those who grew up with it. It's time for some remedial instruction in the use of this global language. Of all the books written on this subject, I nominate *The Elements of Style,* written by William Strunk, Jr. and E. B. White, and published by MacMillan, as the best resource. A periodic review of its compact 85 pages and a catholic reading list of the most accomplished writers in the language will sharpen your writing skills. Also, take advantage of new media such as the Internet and intranets. They will enhance risk management communication. Third, distribute your risk information more widely. Managers will be responsible for relaying information about their risk analyses and organizational risk responses to senior management, and, as well, to the Board, shareholders, employees, suppliers, customers, regulators, lenders and local communities in which your organization operates. Each group has a right to this information. The key lies in knowing how and what to communicate. Remember, too, that risk information flows in both directions. Finally, risk managers will be asked for periodic written and oral reports to senior management and the Board on the overall status of risk. An annual report probably will not be enough. Consider abbreviated monthly or weekly reports. Some financial institutions now call for daily risk reports.

3. **Seize the Opportunity.** My definition of risk is "the possibility of deviation from the expected." Know what is "expected" by each stakeholder group and help each group understand the potential deviations. Risk involves reward and penalty. Prove that the effort of the risk manager results in a favorable risk balance. Become the person in the organization who says, "How can I help you reach that goal?" rather than one who says, "You shouldn't do that." The Chinese

ideogram for risk incorporates both danger and opportunity. Don't overlook one or the other.

4. **Seek New Responsibilities.** Integrated risk management is the future. Whether you call it holistic, business, enterprise or strategic (the term I prefer), balancing risks as a whole, rather than separately, is the challenge. It makes economic sense. Who will take responsibility for this activity? Can you coordinate the initial effort in developing an integrated program? Are you prepared to engineer the joint reporting of all risks? Could you become the focal point for contingency planning and disaster management? I have a sense that contingency planning may become the essence of risk management as organizations recognize that flexibility to meet rapidly changing conditions is the most important organizational attribute. Could you become the "Chief Risk Officer" in your organization, reporting to the CEO and the Board? If not you, who? Many global financial organizations and utilities have already created this position, such as Royal Bank Financial Group, Credit Suisse, Fidelity Investments and Hydro-Quebec. More will follow. The new form of risk management requires new leadership. Be prepared to lead.

5. **Measure Risk Intelligently.** The nature of risk has expanded beyond its traditional two factors of likelihood and potential consequences, both positive and negative. It includes two other critical elements: the public's perception of risk, which may differ markedly from your own or the experts, and the relative confidence you attach to your overall risk assessment. Measurement is becoming more rigorous, with less guesswork. It requires both quantitative and qualitative skills, perhaps with more generous reliance on the qualitative or intuitive. Quantitative tools such as Value at Risk (VaR), Cash Flow Return on Investment (CFROI), RiskMetrics™, Economic Value at Risk (EVA™), Dynamic Financial Analysis (DFA), and Total Risk Profiling (TRP) are sophisticated methods of econometric modeling, but they can create a false sense of security. Avoid an over-reliance on numbers. Learn also the tools of the safety discipline, such as hazard and operability studies (HAZOPS) and fault tree analyses.

    Three of the most valuable books on understanding risk and the tools of measurement are Vernon Grose's *Managing Risk: Systematic*

Loss Prevention for Executives, Peter Schwartz's *The Art of the Long View,* and Peter Bernstein's *Against the Gods: the Remarkable Story of Risk.* Grose approaches the problem from a system safety viewpoint, Bernstein as an economist and finance specialist, and Schwartz as a corporate strategist. Each cautions against over-reliance on numerical quantities and under-reliance on intuition. The first two help managers understand the utility of scenario analyses as keystones for risk assessments. Expand your vision beyond those risks that you were taught and with which you are most comfortable. Look at risks as a whole, at their correlations, and at the consequences, intended and unintended, of your responses. Graphic displays help others to visualize risks as a whole. I've used the Risk Spectrum since 1985: two circles showing global and organizational risks (financial/market; political/regulatory; legal liability, and operational). (For a full copy of the Spectrum, go to www.riskreports.com)

Royal Bank Financial Group, in Canada, uses a pyramid graphic: the top Level 1 for systemic risks, Level 2 for political, reputational, and regulatory risks, and Level 3 for credit, market, operating and people risks.

Understand the entire breadth of risk!

6. **Expand Financial Skills.** Risk managers in the public policy arena often overlook the role that financing plays. Those in financial/ market risk management understand the nuances of derivatives, swaps, options and futures, but they give little credence to other financing tools, such as insurance. Operational risk managers tend to be overly focused on traditional insurance, although many now use the capital markets. Conventional insurance and reinsurance display some glaring weaknesses. Insurers take extraordinary time to complete small tasks, still persist in fragmented underwriting, charge enormous expenses (from 25% to 30% of premiums), offer limited capacity for large exposures, display signs of serious financial instability and give buyers volatility where stability is sought. Risk financing will change dramatically in the next decade, becoming a blend of retention, debt, pooling, capital markets and non-conventional insurance. Peter Bernstein argues that successful risk financing requires a thorough understanding of an organization's

risk appetite (and that includes all stakeholders), liquidity in the marketplace, and the availability of financially secure counterparties. If we can begin to measure risks on a portfolio basis, then we can finance risks in a similar fashion. Implicit in this new paradigm is recognition that traditional "risk transfer" does not exist. The new risk manager understands that risk is only "shared." The risk itself must always remain the responsibility of the creating organization: it can only "share" a portion of that it, plus and minus, with other counterparties. Each will share some of the cost. Over time, the full burden of the reward or penalty of any risk falls on the creating organization.

7. **Understand the Psychology of Risk.** I suggested earlier the importance of developing and understanding of the differing objectives of various stakeholders. Organizations are made up of individuals, internal and external, who display different risk sensitivities, changing daily as new information or pressures appear. Each risk lies in the mind of the observer. Professor Nigel Nicholson, of the London Business School, writing in the July-August 1998 issue of *Harvard Business Review,* in "How Hardwired is Human Behavior?" provides insights into human risk reactions. Evolutionary psychology, he writes, suggests that human beings, while apparently modern, actually retain some ingrained mentality from our Stone Age predecessors. Take the primacy of emotions: "We hear bad news first and loudest." Take risk aversion: "We are hardwired to avoid loss when comfortable but to scramble madly when threatened." On creative thinking: "You can ask people to think outside the box and engage in entrepreneurial endeavors all you want, but don't expect too much. Both are risky behaviors. Indeed any kind of change is risky when you are comfortable with the status quo." On confidence and realism: "The propensity to put confidence before realism also explains why many business people act as though there isn't a problem they can't control: the situation isn't all that bad—all it needs is someone with the right attitude." Professor Nicholson's observations teach us more about the reactions of different stakeholders to risk situations, a critical skill required of future risk managers. These reactions may be ingrained and seemingly irrational, but they will drive risk decisions: try and understand them.

These are a few suggested ideas for the proactive risk managers who will aid their organizations in the next decade. These managers will instill in their compatriots a sense that risk management can never dispose of risk with a magic wand; it can only help us to live with uncertainty more prudently and responsibly. As risks and the tools for treating them change, so too must the risk manager. Do you want to become redundant? Don't change what you are doing!

CHAPTER 4

Risk Management (2000-2004)

*H*ere are four more recent essays, concluding with some simple steps on decision-making under uncertainty.

An Iconoclastic View of Risk
(December 2000)

Challenging the accepted or conventional wisdom is always undertaken with considerable trepidation. Past challengers, like Galileo, Quixote and numerous heretics, met derision or, worse, a flaming stake. Recently we've turned to brainwashing and propaganda to enforce conformity. But the worst fate is probably being disregarded.

I want to attack four serious misconceptions about risk and risk management. Hence the title, "An Iconoclastic View of Risk." Today we know icons more as computer symbols than as the traditional representations of religious persons or images. An iconoclast is one who wants to destroy those symbols. According to the great Arnold Toynbee, in *A Study of History*, "the essence of iconoclasm is an objection to a visual representation of the Godhead or of any other creature, lower than God, whose image might become an object of idolatrous worship." This idea is enshrined in the Second Commandment, which denounces the worship of "graven images," an idea also found in Islam.

I want to extend my personal iconoclastic fury to four "icons" that have grown insidiously and perniciously within our discipline of risk management, icons that, if not broken, may undermine our efforts. They are dangerously subversive.

The four icons that I challenge are the ideas, first, that "risk" is bad; second, that the primary goal of risk management is to benefit shareholders; third, that risk management is the responsibility of specialists; and, fourth, that risk can be transferred.

Icon # 1: Risk is Bad. Why are we so afraid of risk and uncertainty? Consider that the greatest discoveries of the past five centuries have been stimulated by the willingness of explorers, inventors, politicians and scientists to take chances of great loss in return for even greater potential gain. That, to my mind, is the essence of the human spirit, this quest for the new and the unknown. Yes, we are faced by uncertainty whenever we make a decision. The decision itself creates uncertainty as to outcomes. But some of that uncertainty can be measured, thus becoming "risk," and through this measurement we position ourselves to make better decisions, pushing human boundaries outward.

The current problem is the prevailing definition of "risk" offered by some of the risk management sub-disciplines, a definition that is creeping into the vernacular. Safety, public policy and insurance professionals continue to see "risk" primarily as a negative—something to be avoided, reduced or shifted—despite the contrary and broader view of our financial and market brethren. First, this difference confuses those who study the discipline. Second, the more restricted view corrupts responses to risk situations. It forms an artificial blinder constricting perspective. Our ever-increasing ability to measure risk, so thoroughly described in Peter Bernstein's *Against the Gods*, comes to naught if all we try to do is avoid it.

Wiser observers than me have trumpeted that risk and uncertainty are important stimulants for life. ". . . Uncertainty, far from being a symptom of imperfection, is in fact a natural property of economics, indeed, probably of all life systems . . . Uncertainty is the name of the game in the service economy." (Orio Giarini, "The Development of the Service Economy," *Progres,* No. 31, July 2000) Richard Feynman, the Nobel Laureate physicist adds: ". . . it is in the admission of ignorance and the admission of uncertainty that there is hope for the continuous motion of human beings in some direction that doesn't get confined, permanently blocked, as it has so many times before in various periods in the history of man." (*The Meaning of It All,* Helix Books, Massachusetts

1998) And John Adams sees risk as a cultural construct that "illuminates a world of plural rationalities." Risk, to him, is a "balancing act" in which the actors "balance the expected rewards of their actions against the perceived costs of failure" in a world in which both it and our perceptions of it are constantly being transformed by our effect on the world and its effect on us." (*Risk*, UCL Press, London 1995)

It therefore matters how we define risk for our discipline. The November 2000 draft of the ISO/TMB *Risk Management Terminology Paper*, currently under review and discussion, is a step in the right direction. Its authors define risk as "the combination of the probability of an event and its consequence," noting that "consequence may be either positive or negative." ISO adds a footnote suggesting that, "in some situations, risk is a deviation from the expected." That's my preferred definition, one I've been using since 1990. It is brief and it incorporates the positive and negative, the yin and yang, the complimentary opposites, of risk.

Risk always involves a potential reward, whether real or imagined, tangible or intangible. That's why we make decisions involving risk, our personal measure of the uncertainty. To deny the reward element is to distort any subsequent decision. This, to my mind, is why we must break the icon that "risk is bad."

I have three final thoughts on this subject. First, we should acknowledge that not everyone relishes risk and uncertainty as we hope they should. Anthony Storr wrote, "Doubt and uncertainty are distressing conditions from which men and women passionately desire release . . . As a species, we are intolerant of chaos and have a strong predilection for finding and inventing order . . . Certainty is hugely seductive." (*Feet of Clay*, The Free Press, New York 1996) It is the seduction of imagined or promised certainty—the insurance policy that purports to cover everything; the religion that purports to give all the answers—that becomes so corrosive. Yet it is a human response, and one that a risk manager must consider.

Second, risk management, our operational framework, thus becomes "a discipline for dealing with uncertainty," an acknowledgment that both risk and uncertainty are creative stimulants in our lives, and are pervasive. Uncertainty is "the openness of possibility," according to Feynman. Jacob Bronowski phrased it perfectly: ". . . The reality—that, however delicately we work, the random still clings about the systematic, the fluctuations still blur the trend." (*A Sense of the Future,* MIT Press 1977)

And third, I sum up this first icon-smashing effort with a rephrasing of René Descartes' *cogito ergo sum*—"I think, therefore I am." I suggest it should be *periclitor ergo sum*—"I risk, therefore I am." Taking risk is the defining element in human existence. We should relish, not avoid it; balance, not eliminate it.

Icon # 2: The Goal is to Benefit Shareholders. One of the most pernicious current beliefs of risk management is that its sole purpose is to serve shareholders, and to increase share prices. A review of the literature of the last two decades reveals an overwhelming acceptance of this "icon." As one example, the cover of the September/October 2000 issue of *InfoRM,* the magazine of the Institute of Risk Management, worships the idol of "shareholder value." Much of this thinking was spawned by the University of Chicago approach to economics and the undeniable recognition that many corporations became bloated with excessive infrastructure, cheating stockholders of deserved wealth. Yet in the rush to worship the Mammon of share value, we became shortsighted. We've lost touch with the longer-term principles that support survival. If the focus is narrow "shareholder value," how do we then apply risk management to nonprofits, mutual companies, or governmental organizations?

Fortunately, the pendulum is swinging back to common sense. Two recent books support my contention. Allan Kennedy's *The End of Shareholder Value* (Perseus Group, New York 2000) attacks the premise that shareholders are pre-eminent in the pantheon of corporate interests. He suggests that this misplaced emphasis has resulted in unnecessarily large staff cutbacks, a reduction in research and development expenditures, and a misapplication of stock option incentives to senior management, all of which contributed to the current irrational stock market boom. The result: an inevitable reaction from other disenfranchised stakeholders. Employees are no longer loyal to the firm. Suppliers, pressured by demands to reduce costs, reduce services. Customers, seeking only the lowest price, ignore respect for and loyalty to brands. Communities, faced with facilities easily uprooted without notice, respond with restrictive governmental regulations. Kennedy argues that "reconnecting" with these stakeholder groups will be the major mandate for the current decade, as we try and rebuild trust and confidence. Isn't this the primary role for risk management?

The second book is the natural follow-up to Kennedy, John Plender's *A Stake in the Future: The Stakeholding Society*. (Nicholas Brealey, London 1997) Plender asserts the ethical and economic benefits of running a company for the benefit of stakeholders rather than just shareholders. I readily admit that this idea still arouses considerable skepticism, even among economic liberals, but I suggest that it is the coming force.

Risk management's most important role is becoming the mechanism that corrects erratic steering, bringing the vessel back on a principled course. The proper course is to serve all stakeholders, from employees and customers, to suppliers, investors, lenders, regulators, and the community at large. An over-focus on any one set of stakeholders inevitably cheats others. The risk management function has a positive obligation to assess and respond to risks and to develop and maintain a continuing two-way dialogue with every stakeholder group. Our role is not to "reduce the cost of risk," the mantra that has consumed the discipline for almost twenty years, but to enable an organization to build a higher level of confidence and trust within each stakeholder group. That confidence is the most important asset of any organization.

Much of this is recognized by the growing worldwide movement to re-configure organizational governance. It began with the adoption of a new set of risk management standards in Australia and New Zealand and has been followed by the work of the Dey Committee in Canada, the Treadway Commission in the United States, KonTraG in Germany and the Hempel and Turnbull Committees in the United Kingdom. The traditional system of representative governance through a board of directors, governors or trustees does not work. We see the same breakdown in government itself. We no longer trust elected representatives to solve problems, witness the declining participation in national voting, where often less that 50% of the registered electorate actually votes. More and more change occurs because of the money and efforts of special interests lobbying for their perks and because of the outright protests of other groups. The recent debacle in the United Kingdom and Europe over petrol/gasoline prices illustrates this point.

At the corporate level, boards fail to represent broader constituencies than just senior managers and larger shareholders. That is a reason why these commissions have mandated a serious re-structuring of board responsibilities, one of which is the assurance that major risks are understood, assessed and managed. We must move beyond the narrow construction of a director's obligations. I was pleased to see that a financial magazine, *CFO* (October 2000), published by The Economist Group, offered a special award for "managing external stakeholders."

If we accept the principle that risk management, like general management, must serve *all* stakeholders, not just shareholders, it follows that the biggest single responsibility of the risk management function is intelligent communication with these groups. It is also the weakest area of our discipline today. Risk communication should build and maintain the trust of these groups and their confidence in the future of the organization. When this trust is high, the organization's ability to overcome misfortune is enormous; when it is low, no infusion of cash, however large, can save it. The founders of the Global Association of Risk Professionals (GARP), Lev Borodovsky and Marc Loré, wrote, "No matter what types of methods are used, the key to risk management is delivering risk information, in a timely and succinct fashion, while ensuring that key decision makers have the time, the tools, and the incentive to act upon it." (*Risk Professional*, 1999) These "decision makers" include outsiders as well as insiders.

Karen Thiessen, of the Conference Board of Canada, sums it up: "Communicating risks is the process of sharing information about an actual or perceived risk in an open and frank manner. It is essential to building trust with your audience, be it the community, public, employees, shareholders or other stakeholders." (*Don't Gamble with Goodwill: the Value of Effectively Communicating Risks*, Conference Board of Canada, March 2000)

Communication is not easy. Often we deal with stakeholders who lack the requisite knowledge and understanding of issues. Some are fixed on their agendas and don't want to listen or compromise. The experience of Royal Dutch/Shell with environmentalists on the Brent Spar decision arguably led to a conclusion that was worse for the environment than its original proposal of sinking it at sea. We also deal with arrogant and frightened managers—witness the recent problems at Mitsubishi, Ford and Firestone. It will not be easy breaking the instincts to cover up and hide misfortune, or to try and manipulate share price. These are exactly the instincts that proper risk management should work to overcome.

Icon # 3: Risk Management is the Responsibility of Specialists. Over the years, numerous castles of risk management specialization have been erected on the premise that each specialty is so arcane, so based on long experience, that outsiders cannot appreciate, much less practice, the trade. We see this in credit, safety and health, financial derivatives, security, insurance, contingency planning, auditing, contracts and regulatory management. Each group has its own language, its own procedures, its own skill sets. Each wants to be left alone to do the job. Yet this has led to enormous gaps and overlapping and excessive costs in organizational risk responses. The recent move to strategic, integrated, enterprise, or holistic risk management is recognition that the separation of risk functions is actually counter-productive.

Allowing the specialists to ply their trades separately does not work. That is one reason for the rise of a new executive, the Chief Risk Officer. This person is a generalist who reports to both the Chief Executive and the Board—and coordinates the work of other risk specialists. According to a recent global Internet symposium conducted by eRisks in New York, there are almost 200 "CROs" in place, generally in financial institutions, energy and utility companies. They are beginning to adopt common risk languages and frameworks for their organizations. They chair multidisciplinary risk oversight committees and lead new efforts in stakeholder risk communication. Their annual reports now include extensive remarks on both risks and responses. One of the best that I have seen is the 1999 Annual Report from the Bank of Montreal. Taking a full seven of the report's 72 pages, the risk section emphasized the Bank's commitment to *all* stakeholders and described its efforts in credit, liquidity, market and operational risks. At the Bank of Montreal, its CRO is the Executive Vice President who reports to the CEO and chairs the Risk Management Group.

Implicit in the CRO movement is the assumption that risk management is no longer the sole province of specialists. It is now the responsibility of each and every person in the organization. The new goal is to build a culture of risk understanding so that better decisions may be made at every level, every day.

Where will we find these new CROs? To answer this I looked at the various global organizations that represent the risk management discipline. Public policy risk managers belonging to the Society for Risk Analysis and its sub-groups in Europe and Japan number about 4,000. In the insurance arena, the combined worldwide members of RIMS, AIRMIC and their fellow associations in IFRIMA, probably total less than 10,000. GARP, growing rapidly, now has over 13,000 members in 80 countries. Compare these numbers, however, to the 72,000 global members of the Institute of Internal Auditors, and you begin to see how a dramatic predominance of numbers may lead to internal auditors becoming CROs and commanding the risk management discipline. The IIA is shifting its emphasis from its former narrow focus on control to broader and comprehensive risk-based planning in much of its literature, research and training. Given the existing direct contact of internal auditors with boards, we may have an irresistible force.

Icon #4: Risk can be Transferred. Almost thirty years ago, at a luncheon meeting of the board of directors of a major insurance brokerage firm, I suggested the idea that "insurance is a pre-funded line of credit." This heresy met uniform derision as the directors explained that insurance is a risk transfer mechanism. I persisted in my belief, however, coining *Kloman's First Corollary to the Law of Risk Management* in the mid-1980s: "There is no such thing as risk transfer; there is only risk sharing." I believe that risk is created by decisions of individuals or organizations. The potential rewards and penalties accrue to those decision makers. Risk remains their responsibility. Some risk, however, may be shared. An entrepreneur shares both reward and loss with investors who buy stock. Some risk may be diversified. A trader sells a derivative. An insurance buyer shares risk with an insurance company, a pooling of funds given to a fiduciary in return for dispensing them under certain circumstances. Yet most of the risk remains with the original decision maker, and the sharing actually creates a new risk, one that the counterparty may be unable to meet its obligations.

One of the worst fallacies foisted on the public by the insurance industry is that insurance actually solves a risk problem. It does not. It simply provides the possibility of some sharing, some spreading of the risk.

I recently uncovered a classic case of misplaced reliance on insurance. The CFO of a U.S. firm was asked about his organization's dependency on its website and electronic media. The CFO responded: "If the security or privacy of our Website or network were compromised, it would blemish our brand and cause irreparable harm. So our feeling was, let's not spend time thinking about this; let's protect our capital investors and buy an insurance policy." (Russ Banham, quoting the CFO of eCharge Group, *CFO*, August 2000) This attitude not only subscribes to the fallacy that risk can be transferred, it also blindly follows as well Icon Number 2, substituting shareholders for stakeholders. This ostrich-like approach is a patent denial of managerial responsibility.

We must accept full responsibility for the risk decisions that we make. We can find partners with whom to share some portion of the risk, but the final outcome is ours.

The Icons Revisited My objective has been to challenge four serious misunderstandings of risk and risk management. I've tried to shatter some cherished but mistaken beliefs, as a good iconoclast should. If we do not break the icons of delusion that lead us in the wrong direction, toward false gods, we may remain buried in risk illiteracy. If we continue to accept the former "gospel," we may find ourselves mired in a dangerous form of risk management fundamentalism. Risk involves the potential for both reward and harm. The goal is to benefit *all* stakeholders. Risk analyses and responses must be coordinated, and risk is never transferred, only shared. Risk management then becomes, in the words of Sheila Jasanoff of Harvard University, a "framework for learning in the face of uncertainty." ("Between Risk and Precaution—Reassessing the Future of GM Crops," *Journal of Risk Research*, Vol. 3 Issue 3, July 2000)

There is, of course, the possibility that my interpretation is also flawed. That's your challenge: to think seriously about what I have suggested, not just accept it as you may have accepted the previous icons.

I conclude with an appropriate haiku from the Japanese poet Issa. (*One Hundred Famous Haiku*, Japan Publications, Tokyo 1973) He wrote this after seeing an itinerant monk preaching on the side of the road:

> A wayside sermon
> All nonsense to me, but see
> How serene he is!

Enterprise Risk Management:
Past, Present and Future
(May 2003)

Publications, conferences, organizations and vendors constantly trumpet the phrase "enterprise risk management" as if it is the Second Coming or the next great thing since the Internet. Is it a passing fad or can it address some of the pervasive ills that have infected our organizations over the past decade? Do we need the adjective "enterprise" or any of its sister phrases, such as "integrated," "business," "holistic," or "strategic" (which I confess to using)? Isn't all this simply "risk management?" I believe our discipline is important but we must bring it back into perspective. One way to do that is to retrace its historical roots before considering its current posture and where it is likely to lead us. My first step is a short walk through history. Then I describe where we are now, and, finally, I offer some thoughts for the future, as we address three critical management issues.

For me, two authors frame the discussion, pointing out a remarkable paradox. Anthony Storr, in his 1966 study of saints, sinners, madmen and gurus, *Feet of Clay,* wrote that doubt and uncertainty "are distressing conditions from which men and women passionately desire release . . . As a species, we are intolerant of chaos and have a strong predilection for finding and inventing order . . . Certainty is hugely seductive." The human condition does not like uncertainty.

We should like it, however. The Nobel laureate physicist Richard Feynman countered that "it is in the admission of ignorance and the admission of uncertainty that there is hope for the continuous motion of human beings in some direction that doesn't get confined, permanently blocked, as it has so many times before in various periods in the history of man." Progress is dependent on taking risk.

Uncertainty is a human paradox: we fear it but need it! In the past century most corporate, nonprofit and governmental analyses of and responses to both uncertainty and risk were conducted on a fragmented basis. We focused primarily on specific fears and harmful events, looking only at the negative sides of risk to the exclusion of possible benefits. We responded too often to those who had something to sell, financially or politically.

In the future we will look at risks affecting the whole of an organization and its place in the community. We will address both upside and downside consequences and our view will be enterprise-wide, integrated and holistic. The result will be a more intelligent balance between potential benefits and harms. We will increase the confidence of stakeholders in our organizations and make them more resilient in a day and age of increased uncertainty. This is the real goal of risk management.

Where Have We Come From? Human history is a record of attempts to understand unexpected events. Floods, storms, lightning bolts on the one hand, and success in battle and love on the other were all attributed to either the gods or Fate. To avoid misfortune and gain success, men and women prayed to and propitiated gods, singular or plural, including the sacrifice of human beings. Overwhelming uncertainty was the primary fact of life. Later, as we began to keep oral or written histories, we found that some events occur within a pattern. Using this knowledge we built reserves to tide us over when misfortune struck. Farmers allowed their lands to lie fallow once every seven years and took advantage of spring floods. As commerce developed throughout the Mediterranean Sea, shippers wisely split their goods among several vessels to reduce the chance of total loss from weather, pirates or Sirens. Men learned to challenge uncertainty and to determine the causes, other than heavenly wrath, of various misfortunes. They began to create measurable risk from immeasurable uncertainty. This, as Feynman points out, is the essence of humanity: the quest for the new even as we try and explain the old.

Peter Bernstein's *Against the Gods: The Remarkable Story of Risk* is the best chronicle of our centuries-old progress from reliance on the gods to the transformation of some uncertainty into "risk," through the application of experience, numbers and probability. He writes: "The revolutionary idea that defines the boundary between modern times and the past is the mastery of risk: the notion that the future is more than a whim of the gods and that men and women are not passive before nature. Until human beings discovered a way across that boundary, the future was a mirror of the past or a murky domain of oracles and soothsayers who held a monopoly over knowledge of anticipated events."

Bernstein also describes the efforts of well-known trailbreakers such as Pascal, Fermat, Edward Lloyd, Bernoulli, Bayes, and Bentham. He introduces us to many lesser-known names such as Pisano (Arabic numerals), Cardano (probabilities of dice), John Graunt (statistical tables), Abraham de Moivre (the "bell" curve and standard deviation), and Francis Galton (regression to the mean).

But it was the 20th century in which we made the most progress in measuring and understanding risk. Here are some of the milestones:

- Otto von Bismarck introduced social security and workers' compensation in Germany in the late 1800s, from which these ideas spread to Europe and the United States in the early 1900s.

- Frank Knight's *Risk, Uncertainty & Profit* (1921) celebrated the prevalence of surprise and separated risk from uncertainty. He cautioned against over-reliance on extrapolating the past into the future.

- John Maynard Keynes' *Treatise on Probability* (1921) cited the importance of perception and introduced us to the Law of Great Numbers.

- Von Neumann, in 1926, and with Morgenstern in 1953, created the theory of games and strategy and suggested that the goal of not losing is often superior to that of winning.

- Markowitz, in 1952, developed portfolio analysis, including new aspects of returns and variances.

- We formed new associations representing students and practitioners of the discipline, including the Risk & Insurance Management Society (1975), followed by counterparts in Europe, South America, Africa and Asia, the Society for Risk Analysis (1980), London's Institute of Risk Management (1986), the Global Association of Risk Professionals (1996), and the Professional Risk Managers International Association (2002). Older organizations, such as the Institute of Internal Auditors, and the Risk Management Association (formerly Robert Morris Associates), incorporated risk management within their mandates.

- Gustav Hamilton, of Sweden's Statsforetag, created in 1974 a "risk management circle" that first described the interaction and integration of all the elements of the process.

- Daniel Kahneman and Amos Tversky published their "prospect theory" in 1979, demonstrating that human nature can be perversely irrational, especially in the face of risk, and that the fear of loss often trumps the hope of gain.
- The "Precautionary Principle," an idea that first surfaced in Sweden in 1969, was embodied in the U.N. World Charter for Nature in 1982.
- In 1983, William Ruckelshaus, Director of the EPA, gave his seminal speech, "Science, Risk and Public Policy" at National Academy of Sciences, bringing risk analysis to center stage in government and public policy circles.
- Beginning in the mid-1980s, national commissions created new standards and guidelines on risk: the Treadway Commission in the United States, that led to the COSO guidelines (1987), the Cadbury Commission (and following Hempel and Turnbull Commissions) in the United Kingdom (1992), the Australian/New Zealand Risk Management Standard—the first in the world (1995), followed by Canada (1997) and Japan (1997) and the United Kingdom (2001 and 2002).

Where Are We Now? Risk management in 2003 is recognized as an integral part of sound management. It is taught worldwide in more than 100 universities and graduate schools. Yet, because of the continuing inability or unwillingness of many of its practitioners in the separate sub-disciplines to communicate with each other, we lack a common understanding of its meaning.

The word "risk" itself is subject to several interpretations. It can mean "chance of loss," a physical property that is insured, or "a measure of the possibility of unexpected outcomes," the definition that I prefer. The safety, public policy and insurance communities continue to use risk in its limited, negative sense, while financial practitioners see it in its larger sense, encompassing both upside and downside consequences. The International Standards Organization now defines risk as "the combination of the probability of an event and its consequence," noting that "consequence may be either positive or negative." ISO adds a footnote suggesting that, "in some situations, risk is a deviation from the expected." This is a major step forward.

John Adams, in *Risk* (London 1995), sees it as a cultural construct that "illuminates a world of plural rationalities." Risk, to him, is a "balancing act" in which the actors "balance the expected rewards of their actions against the perceived costs of failure" in a world in which expectations and perceptions are constantly changing, in large measure as a result of our multiple responses.

However we define "risk," "risk management" is our discipline for dealing with uncertainty. According to Peter Bernstein, "the essence of risk management lies in maximizing the areas where we have some control over the outcome, while minimizing the areas where we have absolutely no control over the outcomes and the linkage between effect and cause is hidden from us."

Over the years the process of risk management has been encrusted with many overlapping steps, complicating what should be simple. The process has two easily remembered steps: 1) Risk Analysis, and 2) Risk Response.

Risk Analysis includes identification of possible unexpected events, their measurement in terms of likelihood, consequences, and public perceptions, and their assessment in terms of an organization's objectives. Risk Response encompasses the controls adopted to balance risk, measuring and monitoring performance, and communication with stakeholders. The discipline answers the questions "What could happen?" and "What should we do about it?"

Current problems include the often conflicting and confusing "languages" of different practitioners, many of whom are intent on protecting their own traditional "turf," such as derivatives, the environment, health and safety, security, contingency planning or insurance. This inevitably leads to a continued interest in tactical, rather than strategic, responses to risk (buying liability or property insurance; managing currency and interest hedges; reducing employee injuries; protecting environmental resources, etc.) But who is watching the entire store? Cross-turf problems such as the recent examples of outrageous executive compensation and perks, excessively compliant accounting, governance riddled with conflicts of interest, and the failure to communicate intelligently with stakeholders call for a more integrated approach to risk management.

New public accounting and stock exchange guidelines from such diverse areas as North America, the United Kingdom, Germany, India and Malaysia, plus new laws (Sarbanes-Oxley in the United States) create altered responsibilities for governing boards. They must now assure themselves of the depth of risk analyses and the scope of responses.

This in turn stimulated a new executive position in many corporations, the Chief Risk Officer. James Lam created this new responsibility, first at GE Capital in 1993 and later at Fidelity Investments. CROs are now found today in more than 150 major corporations. In addition, in the absence of any group leading enterprise risk management, the internal auditing profession moved into this vacuum, suggesting that its members help create the function. The Institute of Internal Auditors has published several intelligent and practical monographs on the process, conducted numerous global conferences and stimulated new training such as Control Self-Assessment (CSA). It is a natural role for internal auditors, who generally report to both the CEO and the governing board. A question remains, however. Does the practice of risk management conflict with the traditional requirement for auditor independence?

Despite these current problems, I see a growing consensus on the critical steps in risk management:

- Board and senior management commitment
- Broad view of risk encompassing *both* reward and penalty
- Common framework for the integrated analysis of all risks
- Single independent leader or coordinator for the process
- Bottom-up risk assessments, continuing periodically
- Clear and timely data
- Two-way communication with key stakeholders (this is the most often overlooked aspect of today's risk management)
- Creation and maintenance of stakeholder confidence through improving stakeholder "value," creating a healthy internal risk culture

Where Are We Going? I believe that risk management will become a critical part of strategic planning. The sub-disciplines of finance, safety, public policy, insurance, and security, etc. will not only have tactical links, they will also coordinate so that an organization can reach its overall goal of creating and maintaining public confidence. Given that we can never anticipate all possible outcomes in an increasingly volatile world, contingency or business continuity planning will become a major responsibility of the senior risk officer. Finally, organizations will acknowledge that risk management is not the privileged province of specialists but the responsibility of *all* employees. Risk management will become part of the organization's culture.

The greatest area of change will be improvement in communication with stakeholder groups, including employees, customers, suppliers, lenders, investors, regulators, communities and the public at large. It is now risk management's weakest link. When we should communicate? How do we do it? How do we create a two-way dialogue?

In addition, risk management can help organizations solve three major current and future issues:

- *Credibility*: The events of 2001 and 2002, affecting governments, nonprofits and for-profit corporations alike, demand new steps to re-establish stakeholder confidence.
- *Resilience*: Today our organizations are even more vulnerable to the unexpected. How should they prepare? Can they react and survive? Is it time to re-create the idea of redundancies?
- *Perspective*: For too many years corporations, particularly in the developed world, fostered the illusion that an emphasis on short-term results will satisfy their stakeholders. It hasn't worked. We now need to restore the long view and alter organizational culture accordingly.

Why not re-phrase René Descartes' *cogito ergo sum*—"I think, therefore I am?" to *periclitor ergo sum*—"I risk, therefore I am." Taking risk is the defining element in human existence. We should relish, not avoid it; balance, not eliminate it.

Conclusions: Risk management remains a developing discipline, even as it expands to encompass the entire enterprise. It embodies the basic caution that we can never know the future. We can only prepare for it more intelligently. As Steve Hagen concluded in *Buddhism—Plain* *and Simple* (Charles E. Tuttle, Boston 1997): "Underneath the ground of our beliefs, opinions and concepts is a boundless sea of uncertainty." Risk management is the fragile vessel on which we sail this boundless sea. Certainty is always beyond our grasp.

I've been involved with risk management since the mid-1960s, and I admit to a degree of proximity that distorts my own perspective. So I close with two haiku that suggest that my views should be treated with some degree of skepticism and caution.

First, from the poet Bashō:

A cicada shell;
It sang itself
Utterly away

Or, as J. W. Hackett expressed it in another haiku:

Another sermon—
Wafting through words without end,
The smell of coffee!

Australian/New Zealand Risk Management Standard
(November 2004)

Over the past eight years I've commented frequently on the development of "standards" for application to the discipline of risk management (see *RMR* March 1995, February 1996, September 2000, October 2003). It all started with the Australian/New Zealand Risk Management Standard 4360, published in November 1995 and revised in 1999. Standards organizations in Canada, United Kingdom and Japan followed with their own versions and then International Organization for Standardization (ISO) published a glossary of risk management terms in 2001. The Aussies and Kiwis have just finished their latest modification and they've done a superb job again! AS/NZS 4360:2004 was and still remains the clearest and most concise guideline yet published. Its text, only 28 pages, is a model of brevity. It is expressed in simple and basic English, free from business jargon. Because its approach is generic, it applies to all forms of organizations. AS/NZS 4360:2004 will become a handy, notated and dog-eared reference on the desk of anyone who practices this discipline.

Furthermore, as the Standard is generic and requires adaptation to a specific organization, it avoids the complaint that standards are "dangerous" because they can stimulate unneeded legislation and regulations. True, risk management is still evolving, but these guidelines, already in their third evolution, help any organization to begin and modify the process.

The 2004 revision begins with a re-stated section of critical definitions. It goes on to overview and detail the "process," concluding with a three-page description of how to establish an effective program. As with any generic guide, it requires imagination and modification to a specific organization, but this is its beauty. AS/NZS 4360 doesn't tell you how, it tells you why.

The definitions cover most of the words and phrases that appear in risk management literature and are based in large measure on the global ISO/IEC Guide 73 of several years ago. The focus on risk now encompasses unexpected consequences, both favorable and unfavorable. "Control," for example, aims at minimizing negative risk *and* enhancing positive opportunities. "Risk" is defined as "the chance of something happening that will have an impact on objectives," followed by several footnotes refining the idea. One notes that risk "may have a positive or negative impact." Another notes that risk is "measured in terms of a combination of the consequences of an event and their likelihood." "Risk management" is re-defined as "the culture, processes and structures that are directed towards realizing potential opportunities whilst managing adverse effects." This, I'm afraid, remains too broad. Doesn't this definition apply to *all* management? I still think my own wording is closer to what we do: "a discipline for dealing with uncertainty." It's also shorter and easier to remember!

Another change is the elimination of the old entry of "risk transfer," substituting instead "risk sharing," defined as "sharing with another party the burden of loss, or benefit of gain from a particular risk." Bravo! The unexpected outcomes that derive from your decisions must remain your burden or blessing, and only a portion can or should be "shared" with others. The idea of "transfer" creates a false impression that you can shift responsibility and accountability to others. A good example of this is the recent disclosure in *The New York Times* of indemnification agreements between Amtrak, the U.S. government-funded passenger rail carrier, and the freight lines over whose tracks Amtrak operates. In order to use those tracks, Amtrak was forced to sign agreements in which it would indemnify the freight lines for any lawsuits, even those alleging the negligence of the freight lines. For 30 years Amtrak has been paying claims arising out of the obvious negligence of the track owners and they, in turn, must have thought that their risk was truly "transferred." The press disclosure will probably turn the tables and the risk comes back to roost where it belonged in the first place. Risk is never transferred; it is only shared.

Finally, this standard refers to "stakeholders," recognizing the interests of many persons and organizations "who may affect, be affected by, or *perceive* themselves to be affected by a decision, activity or risk." This moves well beyond the restrictive financial focus on "shareholders" or immediate investors, one that has limited the scope of the discipline.

The Standard's process is most notable for its new first step: "communicate and consult." It proposes a "dialogue with stakeholders . . . focused on consultation rather than a one-way flow of information from the decision maker to other stakeholders." I especially like the idea of *starting* the entire process with this step instead of postponing it until after risks have been analyzed and responses adopted. The Standard acknowledges that stakeholder *perceptions* are as important as the estimates of experts and insiders. Other steps (seven in all) include "establish the context, identify risks, analyze risks, evaluate risks, treat risks and monitor and review." I still have some semantic difficulty with the idea of "identifying risk." What we "identify" are the possible unexpected outcomes to our decisions. Risk then is a measure (quantitative or qualitative) of the probable likelihood and consequences of any unexpected outcome. Risk is therefore *analyzed*, not *identified*. Similarly, we do not "treat" risk, we "respond" to it with a variety of mechanisms and further decisions, trying to improve the possibility of more favorable outcomes and reduce the likelihood and consequences of the unfavorable. That's why I continue to prefer a more simple two-step process: risk analysis and risk response, with communication being involved at every level.

These are but minor caveats for a superb statement of the nature and process of our discipline. This document belongs as a *working* guide for all practicing risk managers: don't even think of stuffing it into a bookcase.

> *Risk Management involves managing to achieve an appropriate balance between realizing opportunities for gains while minimizing losses. It is an integral part of good management practice and an essential element of good corporate governance . . . This Standard is concerned with risk as exposure to the consequences of uncertainty, or potential deviations from what is planned or expected. The process described here applies to the management of both potential gains and potential losses.*
>
> **Australian/New Zealand Standard Risk Management**
> **(AS.NZS 4360:2004)**

For a copy of the Standard AS/NZS 4360:2004 and its companion HB 436:2004, a Handbook with more detailed descriptions of applications and approaches, contact Standards Australia at www.standards.com.au or write to them at GPO Box 5420, Sydney, NSW 2001, Australia, or to Standards New Zealand, Private Bag 2439, Wellington 6020, New Zealand.

The Art of Decision-Making
(January 2003)

After many years of personal experience and my thoughtful reading of the wisdom of others, I conclude that making a decision is much less complicated than most make it. It involves five steps:

1. Consider the consequences.
2. Consider the likelihood of those consequences.
3. Consider the odds.
4. Listen to your intuition.
5. Be wary!

CHAPTER 5

Parables

The dream is to find the open channel. What, then, is the meaning of it all? . . . I think we must frankly admit that we do not know.

Richard P. Feynman, *The Meaning of It All*,
Helix Books, Reading, MA 1998

*P*reachers often find parables and analogies useful for illustrating their ideas. I've adopted that approach.

The Parable of the River
(June 2001)

Last month three students of risk management traded emails on the critical starting point of this discipline: how we define our terms. Margaret Davis, of Scotland's Glasgow Caledonian University took issue with two retired codgers, Shaun Wilkinson, the former risk manager of New Zealand's Fletcher Challenge Ltd., and me. With academic care and patience Margaret tried to convince Shaun and me that the meaning of risk is confined to the possible downside of events. We applied our years of experience to argue that it must necessarily involve the potential for both gain and harm. Neither side budged, even though we find that we agree more than we disagree. I thought about her challenge and developed a parable that illustrates the Wilkinson-Kloman point more clearly.

Once upon a time, a man came to a river. It was a quarter mile
wide, with a fast-moving current in its center, tumbling into
dangerous rapids about a mile downstream. His guidebook
warned of piranha both upstream and downstream but not at
his location. He could cross the river easily by walking ten
miles downstream to a bridge. Should he swim across or take
the bridge?

Here is a classic case of decision-making under uncertainty. The man
must weigh his potential rewards with his potential penalties. Yet both
rewards and penalties are contingent on his circumstances at a particular
time. Consider three scenarios. One: he is on a leisurely vacation, with
more than two weeks left. Two: He's at the end of his vacation, with two
hours to catch a homebound plane at the airport just over the river. The
next flight is three days later. His boss will certainly dock his pay if he
returns to work late and may even dismiss him! Three: he's just escaped
from a local jail, where he was tortured and condemned to life
imprisonment. He can hear the pursuing hounds baying in the distance.
Another country lies across the river—with no extradition treaty and
freedom. If he takes the bridge he will be caught.

His risk decision must be based on his balance of both reward and
harm related to the particular time and circumstances. In the first scenario,
he'll detour to the bridge. In the second, the bridge is a probable choice.
In the third, there is no question that he must swim.

What if this man had a corporate staff to advise him? Legal counsel
notes that crossing to the next country other than by the bridge will
constitute illegal entry. Arrest is certain if he swims. Internal Audit argues
that he should wait two days until proper controls can be constructed.
The Human Resources chief is concerned about the potential loss of a
key man. Safety panics: an injury, or worse yet death, would ruin the
safety lost-time record and bring in safety and health inspectors and
regulators. The Insurance Manager reports good and bad news. The good
news is that our traveler is covered by Workers' Compensation and Group
Life Insurance. The bad news is that any injury or death would damage
the loss-premium ratio, bringing higher premiums next year. He too

advises against swimming. By focusing only on the downside *none* of these "risk managers" understand the whole picture!

Extend this parable to a corporate example. A company can invest in a new technology in a new country, guaranteeing a return on equity exceeding 100% for at least the next four years. But the new country (entirely hypothetical) is prone to earthquakes where the plant must be built. Power outages are common every afternoon. And extremists oppose both the plant and its potential product. The country is highly litigious. Class action lawsuits are certain at the first sign of any product fault. A decision must be made immediately as competitors will establish themselves in less than a year if the company fails to act.

Again, the circumstances affect the decision. Scenario One: The company has reported a comfortable ROE of 12% for the past three years, its stock price is steady, and strategists and external analysts consider its prospects good to excellent. Scenario Two: The company's ROE is poor (less than 5% for the past three years), the shareholders and stock analysts are concerned, and some key people are leaving. Scenario Three: The company has reported losses the past three years, cash will run out in less than two years, and it needs a quick and public turn-around to save itself and its jobs.

In the first case, the company weighs the pros and cons and considers the new investment as a joint venture with another organization. In the second it might seek a merger with a larger company with more cash and a stronger bottom line. In the third, it will probably raise as much cash as it can and go for the risky investment. After all, it's somebody else's money!

The moral to these two parables is that any decision made under uncertainty and risk must include the likelihood of *both* rewards and penalties, *plus* consideration of the timing and circumstances. Any risk decision that considers only one side of the equation, be it upside or downside, is incomplete and potentially damaging. To separate the positive rewards, tangible and intangible, from the potential penalties is not risk management.

Yes, Virginia, there is a Santa Claus in risk. A view of risk as a negative corresponds to the pessimistic view of Man as a flawed creature requiring extensive religious or governmental regulation and a continual skeptical view of his actions. I subscribe to the more optimistic view that Man is a creature capable of great good, so long as he has freedom of action. For thousands of years we have endured these antiphonal views of Man, so why should we complain if we have two similar views of risk?

Being on Time
(November 1995)

I will admit to a compulsion about being on time. I arrive at airports a good hour before flight times, and even more for international flights. I champ at the bit if my wife and I don't arrive shortly after the "scheduled" hour for social engagements, even if it means we are usually the first to arrive. When racing sailboats, I want to be on the starting line when the gun sounds, not three seconds late. (Parenthetically I believe that it is important to be over the line early about 5% of the time, a guarantee of well-honed starting skills.) I'm also an admirer of the Swiss railroads. I've timed trains at the St. Gallen station. If the arrival time is 11:04, the train appears in the station at 11:03:30 and stops at exactly 11:04! With this publication, since it has been a monthly, I've delivered my final draft to the printer by the 20th of each month, so that it will be in the mail to subscribers just after the first of each month. It isn't that *RMR* has timely material. It does not. But I want it to be on time.

How did this compulsion occur? I suspect that much of it was instilled by the penalties for tardiness invoked at school and college. Chapel, class, meals and sports: all were run precisely to the clock. It's probably one of the best ways to keep rowdy schoolboys in check. It's also a throwback to the Puritan ethic, with its insistence on not wasting time.

I share my compulsion with many in our modern-day economy, increasingly run on precise timetables and deadlines. Why then are so many of the activities of the insurance industry so chronically late? Renewal quotations arrive just days, if not hours, before renewal deadlines. Policies arrive several months late, and those from London often over a year late. Acknowledgments for letters, faxes, claims take forever.

My diatribe has been stimulated by the senseless procrastination of two insurance agencies involved in a program for which I have some responsibility. In March 1995, I indicated to them that my committee wanted a "stewardship report" on their activities no later than September 1, 1995. This was repeated in May and July. One firm delivered its report on September 5. The second sent a partial report on September 8 and completed it on September 26.

Perhaps these agents believe that time does not exist (see the Borges quote below). Perhaps they have, following Einstein's theories, been able to bend light and compress time, so that September 26 becomes September 1. Not being as skilled, I think I will have to resort to other alternatives to correct the situation.

> . . . the present does not exist, and since the past and future do not exist either, time does not exist.
>
> **Jorge Luis Borges, as quoted in Kenneth Atchity,**
> **A Writer's Time, W. W. Norton & Co., New York 1995**

Interruptions
(November 2000)

Here is the chronic complaint of the aging curmudgeon: When total attention to an event or performance is required, why do interruptions occur? When blissful silence begins to allow a purposeful train of thought to rumble down my track, why is it so mercilessly broken?

Last winter I attended an exceptional concert by Savion Glover, known as the "greatest tap dancer" ever to grace a stage. As I sat mesmerized by his talent, focused on his work and music, my attention was invariably broken by frequent interruptions by the audience, including shrieks of appreciation and applause in mid-performance. It was as if the audience wanted the artist to acknowledge its own presence over and over again. It simply would not allow him to complete a segment unimpeded by applause. The same conditions prevailed in the President's annual State of the Union message before the U.S. Congress this past January: sycophants applauded every phrase with which they agreed, extending the speech to an interminable length. I shut down the television in mid-speech. In this year's debates among those running for the U.S. presidential nomination, whenever a thoughtful candidate paused in mid-phrase for effect or to re-group, his opponents leapt in with their own comments and attacks. Nobody seemed to listen or to want to listen. An intelligent thought could not be completed. One last repository of decorum is the opera: the audience does not yet interrupt Cecelia Bartoli in mid-phrase.

The same occurs at ice hockey, baseball, and basketball games. Whenever the action stops momentarily, or between innings, the arena managers do not believe that we could subsist on silence: they cram every moment with organ music amplified to decibel levels that crush an eardrum. Only English tennis remains a bastion of restraint.

I look forward to my trips by train to Washington, a 5.5-hour break from noise and interruption, when reading, snoozing and thinking are actually possible. Yet even that oasis is drying up amid the onslaught of the cellular telephone. On my last trip I was surrounded by incessant yuppie yakking that destroyed peace and silence. Why is it that they must speak only in the loudest possible voices? Judging from the content, which I could not avoid, little of importance passed through the airwaves. Most speakers appeared to be preening their self-importance.

My point is that we should consider listening a bit more, waiting for the other person to develop and deliver a point, waiting for the artist to complete the expression. We should relish and extend those few moments of relative silence, when reflection occurs. Too often we find silence embarrassing and want to fill it immediately.

There's good news for me, however. With age, hearing diminishes, and hearing aids can be turned off!

> The noise of the world is made out of silences.
> **Theodore Zeldin,** *An Intimate History of Humanity,*
> **HarperCollins, New York 1994**

The Fox in the Henhouse
(August 1998)

In early July my wife brought five laying hens to our home in Tenants Harbor, Maine, for a summer of fresh eggs. Shortly thereafter we flew to Seattle, leaving the hens in the custody of our three granddaughters. On our return, six days later, at midnight, we found the henhouse door wide open and not a hen to be seen. A note from the girls told us that a resident fox had made a meal of each one.

This is a risk management parable. The three girls, during our absence, decided to improve the projected economic return on our investment. They immediately outsourced the management of the production and inventory to a highly qualified consulting and brokerage firm, Reynard & Co., to supervise the hens and their output. The new management team immediately determined that the product was over-priced in the market. Expenses were also excessive: high-cost feed, rental for the henhouse and coop, a sales staff of three, and two senior management, all for a weekly output of 36 eggs. This called for immediate rightsizing and a return of the owners to their core competency, writing and editing. Reynard & Co. then collected its fee up front, and in kind, and returned to its home office looking for similar lucrative assignments, leaving only a few feathers as memories of its work.

The moral: don't let the fox into the henhouse or else you'll find no eggs in your basket.

Nothing's better than dining well on time!

**Homer, *The Odyssey*, translated by
Robert Fagles, Viking,**

Interventions
(April 1997)

Intervention is an expressive word, especially when spoken with a Swiss-German accent. It then becomes "inter-wention" and means that you are being asked to present your iconoclastic views to a group of non-believers. I made my first "inter-wention" to a security conference in St. Gallen, Switzerland in 1977, at the request of Dr. Matthias Haller, then director of the Institute of Insurance Economics at the University of St. Gallen. I've returned to Europe for many similar presentations. After all of these Swiss and German sessions, I received the accolade of knuckles rapping wood, their form of applause.

Intervention has two primary meanings, positive and negative. The favorable one suggests mediation or intercession between two opposing points of view. When that fails, intervention becomes interference and intrusion, resented by all parties. A successful intervention requires acknowledgement of the strengths of respective positions, a cautious disclosure of some weaknesses, and a possible solution born of synthesis. Intervention is diplomacy married to direction.

This word reappeared not because of another call from Dr. Haller but because of a challenging short piece by John Barth, in *The New York Times Magazine*, on March 9, 1997, entitled "Inventing a Few More Tomorrows." Barth wrote, "But one's calling is intervention, not confession." My calling in this publication is intervention. The path is not smooth. I often stumble, but I hope to intervene and suggest alternatives not previously considered. Avoiding pitfalls isn't easy. Some pitfalls are generalities: *The Economist* unloaded on President Clinton's 1997 state-of-the-union speech, saying that "he descended to the occasion, peddling treacly generalities." I occasionally must plead guilty to sentimentality, a product of advancing age. Another pitfall: while experience brings perspective, retirement distances an observer from day-to-day action, and what I find appropriate may be impractical for troops in the field. As Salman Rushdie wrote in *Midnight's Children*, ". . . above all things, I fear absurdity."

So treat my interventions with both deference and skepticism!

Micromanaging Minutiae
(October 1996)

Shouldn't those who practice risk management devote the bulk of their attention to risks that are truly material to their organizations? If we agree on this, why do so many persist in micromanaging minutiae?

The fundamental problem facing risk managers who are involved in insurance matters is that they over-focus on relatively mundane problems. They manage minuscule risks—slip-and-fall lawsuits, auto accidents, loss of personal computers; workers' compensation accidents, etc.—overlooking more serious risks. They seem to relish the management of claims, not the management of risk. Why do they choose the relatively trivial? The answer is easy: insurance. These claims are conventionally covered by property and liability insurance and insurance dominates the picture. Insurance underwriters prefer to underwrite the predictable and the recurring, avoiding the potentially massive and less predictable. They can generate handsome profits (if not underwriting profits, then investment income) on these losses without risking big hits. Yet these are the very same losses that most organizations themselves can easily afford to fund internally. If a risk management program is anchored in insurance, these minor risks prevail, leaving no time to study major risks.

Consider the annual RIMS/Tillinghast Cost of Risk Survey numbers: the total cost of insurable risks is well under 1% of revenues for most organizations. Why bother with insurance? Why not dispense with the high time requirements of annual insurance renewals, bid reviews, policy evaluations, claims filings and follow-ups, and the need to work through an outmoded system of intermediaries.

Smaller risks, losses, and claims need management, but shouldn't they be the responsibility of local operating managers who control them in the first place? Corporate risk managers can provide some counsel and advice but should not become mired in tactical details.

If those who call themselves "risk managers" want to provide significant service to their organizations, they should look first at *all* risks, whether operational, liability, regulatory/political, or financial/market, and begin with those most influencing finances and reputation.

The old insurance/risk management function was organized along the lines of insurance: property, crime, marine, liability, and workers' compensation. The new strategic risk management function will be organized along process lines: risk assessment, risk control, risk financing, and communications.

I am the first to admit that it is often difficult to identify a "major" risk. This past summer, a perfect example occurred in Maine. The DeCoster Egg Farms, a conglomerate that supplies a large percentage of fresh brown eggs to New England supermarkets, was hit with $3.6 million in fines from the Occupational Safety & Health Administration for deplorable working and living conditions at its farm in Turner, Maine. Each citation in and of itself might have been considered minor, and even the fine, while large, might have been the end of the affair if the owner has responded immediately with a "mea culpa" and a promise to rectify the situation. The response, however, was vague. Press attention followed, along with public pressure and a boycott by many of New England's major supermarkets and retail chains—stores that accounted for almost 20% of the farm's sales. The ensuing financial effects and damage to reputation forced a much more costly response, and the boycotts will probably continue until independent assessors confirm promised changes.

As risk managers look to their more significant risks, they should be aware of the potential ripple effects from smaller events, especially those that affect reputation. If they continue to "micromanage minutiae" they may overlook the sequence of events that shook DeCoster, just as they are likely to overlook a Leeson (Barings) or a Citron (Orange County) manipulating investments. The risk manager must take a broader, more strategic view of risk.

Desecration of the House
(March 1997)

Occasionally I will watch on television, with muted sound, a rendition of Canadian folk opera, listening to more civilized background music. On a February evening it was Beethoven (hence the title) and the New York Rangers visually committing mayhem on a lesser National Hockey League opponent. Even the muting of sound advertisements didn't do the job: I was bothered by losing sight of the puck along the boards, buried by advertisements. Every inch of vacant space, once white, was covered by pleas to purchase beer, stocks, automobiles, hamburgers and even insurance. Despite the coverage of the commercial breaks by Ludwig, commercialism continued to detract from the game.

We're engulfed by commercialism. Is it possible that Beethoven's *Calm Seas and a Prosperous Voyage* was commercially sponsored? I can imagine a German marine insurance company commissioning that work. Everywhere we look, the forces of the market thrust their wares on us. The Seattle, Washington high schools now sell advertising space on their buses, team uniforms, walls, and schoolbooks just to gain extra dollars.

The operators of the infamous Channel One "give" VCRs and television monitors to classrooms in return for blasting children with plugs for products, embedded within the "news." Nonprofit organizations endorse credit cards, telephone companies, automakers and insurance schemes in return for more income. Golf tournaments, once identified by their locations, are now "classics," modified by commercial sponsors. At risk management conferences, we're given tote bags endorsing insurance brokers and asked to attend breakfasts, lunches and dinners where plugs precede food.

When, as resident curmudgeon, I've complained, I'm told that I should be a realist. The only way to survive, I'm advised, is to accept commercial sponsorship. The ends justify the means! Taxpayers won't pay for education or for the debts of their governments. Association members resist dues that would eliminate commercial endorsements. Conference attendees actually seem to like the volume of twaddle that washes over them, reducing their registration fees. Entire channels of television are now devoted to infomercials, 24 hour selling of over-priced products.

I acknowledge the role that public presentation of commercial products and services plays in a market economy, but does it have to be so pervasive? It's a sign of the times—a willingness to let someone else pay, even though it begins to distort what we enjoy. Can electronic wizards develop some chip that will erase advertising from hockey boards and skip quietly and blankly over the "commercial intervals?" Will a consumer backlash shift support to public television channels that seem to be slipping into the commercial morass? Will registrants at conferences pay a fair price for a session devoid of commercialism? Wishful thinking.

In the meantime, I'll continue to rail against this monster, and listen to the masters while watching Canadian folk opera.

Crime, Computers and Women
(December 1996)

Seventeen days of travel to California and Washington gave me a fresh appreciation of certain aspects of risk management. Insight comes from new perspectives.

First, take crime. We complain vigorously about the frequency and severity of lawlessness, in spite of recent reductions in criminal activity. We read the headline stories of drive-by shootings, office assaults, molesters preying on children, and scams defrauding the aged and the unwary. Our national consciousness of our criminal propensity has stimulated both police and better policing. I saw an example of this walking along the Oakland Estuary one afternoon. A group of thirty police officers, all clad in shorts, were learning how to handle mountain bikes in preparation for their duties in neighborhood law enforcement. They appeared reasonably fit, hardly the stereotype of the overweight policeman. I stopped to talk with one officer. He explained that being on bicycles made police officers more approachable than when in cars, while still having mobility—both important pieces of neighborhood policing, the newest idea in crime prevention. Isn't this a return to the basic precepts of Sir Robert Peel and his "bobbies" in England in the 19th century? Nevertheless, the bicycle police officers of Oakland were a refreshing example of an innovative response to crime.

Second, consider computers. The pages of computer and software advertising in U.S. newspapers are clear evidence that this new technology has enveloped our lives. Ten years ago, my family had no computers at home; today we have four: an Apple Mac Performa for this publication, an unused Mac Powerbook, a Compaq that my wife uses for transcribing in Braille for the blind, and her Mac SE, comparable to a Model T Ford, on which she writes her novels. My fresh look at the computer generation came from a lunch with my personal computer guru, Allen Munroe, in Larkspur, California. Allen is far more computer literate. He manages one of the best risk management Web sites: http://www.riskinfo.com. It's also the *Risk Management Reports* site, where you can find electronic copies of all of the 1996 issues of *RMR*. RiskInfo houses other publications, like *Practical Risk Management* and *Smart's*, a review of the California insurance scene, as well as an on-going *RiskForum*. I acknowledge that I am still scratching the surface of the new medium of the Internet and that Allen is light years (or at least five years) ahead of me. He reminds me that our rapid transition into an information economy carries with it increased uncertainties as well as awesome opportunities.

We tend to overlook the risks, fears and uncertainties inherent in a major technological, economic, and social revolution, lured by its promised riches. Jobs will be destroyed, but new ones will spring up. On my flight west I read the World Market Survey in *The Economist* ("The Hitchhiker's Guide to Cybernomics," September 28, 1996). Allen's forecasts reminded me of the costs as well as the benefits of this transition to an information technology society.

What will happen to our old-fashioned knowledge dispensers: lawyers, accountants, consultants, insurance agents and brokers? Are they destined to become "the modern counterparts of weavers, whose incomes soared after spinning was mechanized, only to crash when new machines emulated their own craft?" If the Internet, through Web sites and discussion groups, can provide immediate and continuous access to peers and specialists, do we need to hire these service providers at their outrageous fees? If we can reach banks, insurance companies, and capital markets through the Internet, why pay high commissions to intermediaries?

The Economist's answer: the lazy, slow and less educated will suffer the fate of the weaver; the well-educated will survive and prosper.

Will the computer, as everyman's access to the infinite world of information, condemn to oblivion the idea of the firm, the corporation, the gathering of numerous people in one location in joint pursuit of profit? Do we need these "artificial" groups when networking can be more efficiently achieved individually? This is infinite outsourcing! Employees, or better yet, independent contractors, can be linked through electronic networks.

Allen Munroe was encouraging. Despite my relative ignorance of the electronic marvels of the information age, he assured me that I could learn (and that they will be simplified to meet the deficiencies of technologically-challenged Neanderthals like me). He reminded me, however, that I still must try to keep pace with this revolution. As *The Economist* concluded in its survey, knowledge—finding better ways to do things—has always been the main source of long-term economic growth, from the agricultural revolution to the present day. What is different this time? "First, IT (information technology) has accelerated the shift towards a knowledge-based economy by allowing more information to be codified in digital form, making it easy to transmit over long distances at low cost. Second, production is increasingly in the form of intangibles, based on the exploitation of ideas, rather than material things."

Where once land, physical property, and financial resources were critical assets, now knowledge is the fundamental asset. The computer is our access to that knowledge.

Third, watch women. I attended (in the real sense of the word, as "attendant") my wife's 40th reunion of her graduation from Mills College, in Oakland, California. Mills remains a women's college, even though it has, from time to time permitted a few especially qualified men as graduate students in its arts programs (Darius Milhaud and Dave Brubeck are two who attended Mills when my wife was there in the 50s). These ladies, forty years on, were as exuberant, independent, and staunchly feminist as I remembered them in 1956, when I first went to its eucalyptus-scented campus. Their battles and victories against the curtain of male corporate exclusivity (and pomposity) remind me that we still have some way to go before the extraordinary capabilities of women are fully realized in our economy. Even the most rigorous religious restrictions did not prevent women like Golda Meir, Indira Gandhi and Benazir Bhutto from leading their countries, and in Europe and North America women's political progress has been greater. It also reminds me that, as progress is being made, the failures to open opportunities will become more costly, in terms of both litigation and lost resources.

Personal Risk Analysis
(December 2004)

After laboring through the lengthy descriptions of how to undertake risk analyses, freighted with the business jargon and multi-syllabic words found in many of the new guides and books, I decided that I should try and apply some of the more coherent principles to my own decision-making, as a test case. Would this analysis change a habit or, at least, lead to modifications that improve the potential for favorable results and reduced potential harms?

I selected a decision that I have made every morning between 0700 and 0800 over the past decade. It is my daily trek from the house, across the field and down the drive—a distance of about 150 yards roundtrip—to collect my morning newspaper plus yesterday's mail if George was late, as he is perhaps once a week. Given some travel and a few months each year in Maine, I've made this walk—about 3.5 minutes elapsed time—more than 2800 times, so I have a database of significance in my memory.

First, what are my expected benefits and their probabilities? They include a breath of fresh air, a modest stretch of the legs, plus the news, sports scores and comics during breakfast. We'll just accept all these as intangible and not try and attach a financial value to each. Based on my ten year history, the probability of enjoying these expectations is very high. What about unexpected favorable outcomes? About once a week, I have the chance of saying a cheery good morning to a passing neighbor: a likelihood of .14. Or I could find a very large check in the mailbox—a miniscule likelihood (it hasn't happened in all these years, but it could).

Now, let's balance these purported benefits with the potential for expected and unexpected harms. Once a month, the paper isn't there (they failed to print, a blizzard intervened, a slippery-fingered neighbor lifted the paper)—a .033 probability, but it permits me to explode with a few choice words about the unreliability of life in general which, in turn, is probably a psychological benefit to me, if not to anyone within hearing distance. Nothing else untoward has happened in these years but, as we are warned, IT COULD! If the snow is deep, I must take additional time to don boots; if it is raining, a raincoat. A sudden downpour might soak me. A speeding car could dispatch me to never-neverland, although we generally have only fifteen vehicles an hour on this country road. A bolt of lightning could strike, a tree limb could fall, a tornado might arrive just as I leave the house, or a tidal wave could roar up the Connecticut River and Lord's Creek, engulfing Ely's Ferry Road, the mailbox and me. Probabilities? Miniscule, although the consequences might be terminal! More likely, I could trip and fall in a mole hole or be attacked by one of these ravenous and even rabid rodents sent across the street by a parsimonious neighbor who can't seem to provide properly for his animals. My mind boggles at the downside possibilities. No wonder people become risk averse!

Ah but, the risk manager says, we can construct controls that will limit these destructive forces. What are my options? I can check the thermometer before going out so that I am properly dressed: cost—about 30 seconds. I could cancel my paper subscription, saving $120 a year, but the intangible cost—missing the comics and the Red Sox scores—more than offsets those savings. Finally, I could screw up my courage and ask my wife and copy editor to get the paper for me, saving 3+ minutes of my more valuable time. The costs of this option, however, in potential negative consequences are "beyond category," as they say about the steepest Alpine climbs in the Tour de France!

My risk analysis is complete. I've weighed the likelihood of positive and negative consequences of my daily decision to fetch the paper. I think I'll continue as before, keeping a weather eye out for those damn moles.

> *The predictable becomes, by definition, background, leaving the attention uncluttered, the better to deal with the random or unexpected.*
>
> **Ian McEwan,** *Enduring Love*, **Random House, New York 1999**

Chocolate
(February 1999)

At the end of January, I exhausted the supply of quality chocolate that arrives each year with Christmas. Sad and stuffed, I face eleven lean months using my own funds to feed my craving until the gift-giving season returns. I've worked my way through L.A. Burdick bars crammed with nuts, through Lindt and Scharffen Berger bittersweet, whose aroma and taste invoke the praise that accompanies fine wines. I've indulged with my favorite, Green & Black's Organic Dark, "conched" from whole cocoa beans expressly grown in Togo for the company. Its 70% cocoa marks it as some of the finest plain chocolate in the world. I first bought it in London and later ordered it in case lots of 24 bars from a small shop in New York. Now a local environmental food store in Niantic feeds my habit.

Until this year, my chocoholic tendencies were accompanied by guilt, as I tried to refrain from the delicacy. But just after Christmas a fax arrived proclaiming: "We Are Saved! The Lord Has Spoken! Hallelujah!" It contained a clipping from that day's issue of *The New York Times*. Apparently a research study of 7,841 Harvard male (why were women excluded?) graduates, made by the Harvard School of Public Health and published in *The British Medical Journal*, found that consumption of chocolate may extend one's life! (Of course, we chocoholics knew that but were unwilling to share this information with others for fear that the supply of this life-giving commodity would be in jeopardy and the price would rocket upwards.) Now the secret is out. Chocolate apparently contains phenols, the same antioxidant chemicals found in wine that prevent fatty substances from oxidizing and clogging the arteries.

So doctors may now prescribe chocolate, at least for men. Company cafeterias can serve it daily, and risk managers can encourage its use. The risk of an expanded waistline is now more than offset by the benefit of a longer life! I am a believer!

CHAPTER 6

Sports Analogies

It helps from time to time to use an analogy from the sporting world to explain to and instruct others in some of the more intricate details of our discipline. As I have been an ice hockey player, rower and sailor for many years, the following analogies came easily to me. Yes, solitaire and crossword puzzles are also forms of sport!

Varnishing
(September 1994)

Sailors who move about in wooden boats belong to a different breed. I understand this because I have two friends who persist in maintaining yachts that require enormous quantities of elbow grease and time in the annual re-varnishing of their brightwork. My plastic boat, with a minimum of wood to varnish, is derided by the woodies as a "clorox bottle." But I am sailing early in the spring, while they labor on spars and teak trim into the hot days of July. Of course, their boats *are* beautiful, but at what expense? Have they developed benefits that more than compensate for their lost sailing time? Perhaps pride in results and the cultivation of patience are their rewards. I've observed that these attributes are carried forward into their business attitudes, and their businesses are the better for them. They sacrifice immediate gratification for the beauty of their results, their pride in them, and the development of the admirable trait of patience.

All of this was reinforced after reading Rebecca Wittman's *Brightwork*, a psalm to varnishing and the art of finishing wood (International Marine

Publishers, Camden, Maine, 1990). It is literally a glowing tribute (the pictures are magnificent) to the beauty of carefully varnished brightwork on boats. Throughout her work, Ms. Wittman emphasizes the need for utmost patience. And when I read her "ten commandments" for yacht refinishing, I was struck by how appropriate they are for those of us who practice the discipline of risk management. These are my paraphrases of her commandments:

1. **Honor thy yacht:** Proper respect for your organization, its products and services, its people, its suppliers and customers, and its communities—in a word, its stakeholders—is essential for sound risk management.

2. **Thou shalt not tempt Mother Nature:** A thoughtful risk manager recognizes the external forces at work on the organization and is not too rash. Just as it is foolish to varnish before rain, it is inappropriate to locate a facility in a flood plain or earthquake-prone area. If you deliberately challenge Mother Nature, she will nail you sooner or later.

3. **Be neat in thy work:** Sloppy work takes less time but the results are all too evident. Take time to create and maintain clear and coherent records. Don't rush your work because of the unrealistic deadlines of others.

4. **Understand thy chosen finish:** Study carefully all possible responses to risk, ranging from avoidance and mitigation to various forms of financing. Assure yourself of the best "finish" or combination of "finishes."

5. **Do thy product research:** Know the pros and cons of services and service providers, such as risk assessments, actuarial analyses, technical controls, claims services, and insurance contracts, enabling you to use them confidently and know what to expect from each one.

6. **Know thy hardwoods:** Make sure that you know your own organization as well or better than anyone else. Understand its people, its products, services, and facilities. Don't compromise by accepting the opinions and views of others: go forth and see for yourself—often.

7. **Neglect not thy detailing:** When reports, analyses, papers, and contracts pertaining to risk management are prepared, make sure that you read and understand them. Don't depend on the analyses of others. Study risk assessments and read insurance contracts, tedious as this may be.

8. **Keep thee safe and alive:** Self-preservation is important, in terms of both physical safety and health and the function of risk management within the organization. Practice the risk controls you preach. Stress the importance of risk and loss control.

9. **Keep the preventive maintenance creed:** Preemptive action is the ounce that easily outweighs the pound of cure required later. Early action generally prevents paying more for later losses.

10. **Thou shalt love working on thy yacht:** Some years ago, Tom Peters noted that many leaders of highly successful companies shared a distinguishing characteristic: their "love of product." If you don't enjoy risk management work, seek another line. Your lack of passion will show up quickly, like a dull finish from sloppy varnishing.

Above all, be patient. Changes take time because large organizations are hard to move. Entrenched bureaucracies, common to government, corporations, and services, protect their own systems, but persistent pressure will, over time, produce favorable results.

Having patiently sanded and applied eight coats of varnish to my own boat's handrails over a two-week span, carefully watching the temperature and humidity, cleaning my brushes, and using only the best varnish, I am proud of the results. They will last. So will your risk management results if you follow Ms. Wittman's suggestions.

Skills and Aptitudes
(May 2004)

What are the skills we need in the future? I heard this question twice in the past eight months, first from a parent of a young sailor enrolled in a sailing program in Tenants Harbor, Maine, and later from a risk manager in Seattle, Washington. The answer, I think, is found not so much in specific skills as in aptitudes.

Take sailing, for example. The skills that are required to handle a small boat successfully in various types of weather and sea conditions include being able to swim, knowing the parts of a boat and its rigging, understanding how sails work, sailing a boat both upwind and downwind, knowing what to do in the event of a person overboard or a capsize, leaving from and returning to docks, mooring, tying the correct knots and understanding weather, tides and currents. These are specific and necessary skills that are easily taught. More significant, however, are the aptitudes that serve as the foundation for these skills. Independence is the first: the willingness to step out on your own. Patience is the second: understanding that a sailboat cannot go directly upwind, nor can it move when there is no wind. And third is teamwork: sailing and racing a small boat requires exquisite timing and cooperation in order to do well. Without these three aptitudes, a sailor literally may be at sea.

My sailing analogy applies equally to the aptitudes necessary in the discipline of risk management. Again, independence comes first. In its current evolution as an integrated and strategic process throughout any enterprise, its "champion" and guide *must* be independent of conventional staff and operating functions. Too many organizations attempt to force risk management into finance where it becomes both dependent and restricted. Independence begins with a fresh and broader view of "risk" itself. It is not, as too many safety, finance and insurance practitioners construe it, merely a "chance of loss." It must be viewed as encompassing the unexpected, both favorable *and* unfavorable. Risk is "a measure of the possibility of unexpected outcomes." Under this definition risk management becomes "a discipline for dealing with uncertainty"—a far more strategic approach than as construed by the narrow confines of finance, insurance, safety, quality control, and business recovery planning. Risk management independence thus requires a leader who has a direct reporting relationship to *both* the CEO *and* the organization's governing board. Only in this way can that leader raise unpopular and even dangerous risk issues—those risk issues that are truly material to the future of the organization.

As an example, the most pressing current issue is that of excessive executive compensation. Too many organizations have allowed their senior management reward systems to skyrocket to obscene levels. CEOs are naturally unwilling to take action and compliant boards exacerbate the problem. The result: regulators, shareholders and stakeholders lose confidence in management. We need chief risk officers who are both able and willing to address these and similar larger strategic issues and who, at the same time, can present these issues intelligently and dispassionately to critical board committees. Otherwise, we will continue to focus on relatively minor risks to the exclusion of those that materially affect our futures. As David Godfrey, the CRO for Swiss Reinsurance Company, said recently, "And from time to time you (the CRO) need the ability to say, 'I'm sorry, but I don't agree with what you say.' If you (the CRO) only report to the CEO, it's very difficult to go beyond that in order to express disagreement, if the channels aren't there already to do so." (See "ERM, Operational Risk and Risk Management Evolution," in *GARP Risk Review,* March/April 2004)

Lesley Daniels Webster, the Executive Vice President and Global Head of Market Risk at JPMorganChase, echoed this theme when she emphasized the necessity of a CRO having the "willingness and ability to criticize senior and operating management when required" (her speech at the GARP 2004 Conference, February 25, 2004).

The Economist stated the issue of trust and independence most succinctly in its April 22, 2000 issue: "There may be two good reasons for companies to worry about ethical behavior. One is anticipation: bad behavior, once it stirs up a public fuss, may provoke legislation that companies will find more irksome than self-restraint. The other, more crucial, is trust. A company that is not trusted by its employees, partners and customers will suffer."

Independence of risk management is necessary to permit and stimulate both strategic perspective and the courage to speak out when required. It is an aptitude that transcends specific skills.

The second aptitude, drawn from sailing, is patience. When the wind isn't favorable, you may have to anchor and wait for it to change. For centuries, the Chinese used bamboo as a comparable example. In a storm, the bamboo shaft bends but doesn't break, springing back to its normal position when the winds subside. Patience implies a long-term view of an organization and its future. One of the most pernicious current problems is the over-focus, even paranoia, on "shareholder value" and near-term stock prices. We have succumbed to a mass frenzy trying to outdo each other in managed earnings and artificial stimulation of the daily prices posted in New York, London, Frankfurt and Sydney. The patient CRO understands the long-view of an organization's responsibility to its stakeholders, including shareholders, one that may reach out as far as twenty to thirty years. Patience means revising the goal of risk management (and the organization itself) to "building and maintaining stakeholder confidence." Shareholder value is but a piece of this equation, with all respect to the University of Chicago theories of economic practice.

If a CRO accepts this basic thesis, then it follows that the three basic objectives of risk management must be:

- Credibility: Communicating the nature of risks, both favorable and unfavorable, with stakeholders, and their responses, to enhance the support of these groups for the organization.
- Resilience: Building an internal and external flexibility so that the organization can respond to whatever unexpected event may occur—and in many cases actually taking advantage of a downside event to improve market position.
- Perspective: Countering the prevailing over-focus on the short-term. Here Peter Schwartz's *The Art of the Long View* (Doubleday, 1991) remains one of the best expositions of long-term perspective.

Patience, however, has an Achilles Heel. Most of the prevailing metrics for measuring the success or failure of a risk management function are cast in short-term numbers. VaR is one of these, and it, similar to many others, is flawed. No one has yet developed a consistent and accepted metric for measuring the longer-term results of risk management. We need one, and we may be condemned to the short-term until and unless we can create a new measure.

The third aptitude is teamwork. Because tactical risk management embodies so many different skills, it makes good sense for its practitioners to reach out and try and understand the problems and solutions of others. While we are making some progress within organizations toward breaking down the artificial barriers that kept us from communicating with one another, too many of our major associations of risk management players continue to operate behind impregnable fortresses. Most are unable, even unwilling, to bring representatives of their counterpart groups to their annual conferences and local chapter meetings. The result is an appalling lack of knowledge of the work of others. Last December, I asked an audience of some 40 members of the Society for Risk Analysis how many had even heard of GARP, PRMIA or RIMS. Two hands were raised. I questioned registrants at the February 2004 GARP meeting: few had heard of SRA or RIMS. Then, at a RIMS chapter meeting in Seattle in March, I asked the same question of over 100 registrants. Only one was also a member of GARP; none were members of PRMIA or SRA. Many members of one association had not even heard of the other groups. This is the worst sort of parochialism.

Many specialist skills are required for risk analysis—the first step in the process (the identification of possible unexpected events; their measurement in terms of likelihood, timing, consequences and public perception; and their assessment relative to an organization's objectives). They include scenario analysis, quantitative and probabilistic analysis, actuarial science, data management, knowledge of the law, econometric modeling, intuition and the use of heuristics, and, of course, the value of experience. Similarly, another set of skills is employed in risk response— the second step in the process (controls adopted to balance upside and downside risk; measuring and monitoring performance; and communicating with stakeholders). These skills include knowledge of safety and quality systems (Six Sigma), audit and accounting controls, environmental controls, behavioral economics (financial incentives and penalties), contingency and crisis management (business recovery planning), and financing (credit, derivatives, hedging, pooling, use of capital markets, insurance and claims management). It is too much to ask any one person to be fully conversant and expert in *all* these fields. This makes teamwork *the* mandatory aptitude. It is high time that the IIA, GARP, PRMIA, RMA, CAS/SOA, SRA, RIMS/IFRIMA and ASSE, among others, cease their guild-like restrictiveness and reach out to their counterparts, expanding the scope of our discipline.

Swiss Re's David Bothwell addressed the question of skills in a similar fashion: "They (risk officers) have to have skills that are seen to be relevant and at a high level. They have to be seen to be balanced, to look at the total picture, assessing the opportunity which the deal-doer is telling you is the greatest thing since sliced bread . . . while at the same time balancing that with the broader picture. They have to be able to articulate well their reasoning for a particular position or view-point . . . they have to be consistent—or they will lose respect . . . But in the final analysis, they ultimately have to be prepared to stand up and say no."

The major challenge for any risk management team is the prevailing failure to communicate intelligently and coherently with all of our stakeholder groups. In *RMR* (April 2004), I described the Bank of Montreal's exceptional eight-page summation of its internal risk management program. Too few organizations attempt this. I know of no organization that employs a consistent and effective continuing two-way dialogue with its stakeholder groups on its analysis of risks and its responses. Perhaps improved teamwork among the existing risk management groups can develop a better means of communication.

Academic institutions are a critical part of the teamwork equation. More are beginning to stretch their formerly narrow programs (finance; insurance; public policy; engineering) to incorporate ideas and methods from the other sub-disciplines. I hope that many of the association-run certification programs will also acknowledge their competitors and expand their curricula to include, as least nominally, other ideas and techniques.

Independence, patience and teamwork are three critical aptitudes for those who purport to practice this evolving discipline of risk management. Within them one can develop other technical skills; without them, these skills are meaningless.

Problem Solving
(November 2003)

I'm always intrigued with the machinations of the human mind, especially when it comes to solving problems. For more than fifty years I've been addicted to crosswords, slowly gaining an expertise that now allows me to complete at least the Monday through Thursday puzzles in

The New York Times. On Fridays and Saturdays I require the help of my copy editor, and we share Sunday's longer puzzle.

Friday, June 27, 2003 was a typical day for me with a difficult puzzle. I started after lunch on our porch in Maine, making little progress during the first half-hour. The page showed numerous "s" and "ed" endings plus a few lightly penciled guesses (I use a pen for Monday through Wednesday, shifting sensibly to a pencil for the harder late-in-the-week puzzles). Then a phone call derailed me for the afternoon. I returned to the project at 5 p.m., with a tot of rum to stimulate the senses, completing the top left and bottom right in twenty minutes, after which I found myself stymied again. I put the puzzle aside a second time.

The Boston Red Sox intervened after dinner, but they scored ten runs before an out, going on to fourteen runs in the first inning. With the game's conclusion foregone, I picked up the puzzle, finishing in twenty minutes all but the upper right-hand corner, which continued to be incomprehensible. Finally, at 9:30 p.m., after an hour of reading, I finished it off with ease in less than ten minutes, wondering why what was so obvious then had been so difficult earlier. My elapsed time: 80 minutes of struggle. Not world-class but, like the tortoise, I *did* finish.

The point of this tale is that the human mind works strangely. By bringing a fresh and uncluttered mind to bear at different times, we can more readily solve difficult problems. A judicious pause or break can refresh our ability to untangle the knots. Is this a new insight? Hardly, but the message requires repetition, especially in a world that wants immediate results. Good work takes time and repeated assaults.

I learned a variation on this theme while serving in the U. S. Navy in the mid-1950s. One evening at sea, closing the coast of Japan, I stood on the bridge with the ship's navigator searching the horizon for the flash of a lighthouse that marked a major course change. We knew it would be just off the port bow. The navigator suggested that I would have better luck in sighting the light if I looked not directly at the point where I expected it but to either side of that point, using my peripheral vision. It worked. I spotted the light before the lookouts, and I learned a lesson in both physics and human nature. We often reach objectives not through direct approaches but through the indirect.

I use both approaches for writing and editing *Risk Management Reports.* If I try and create ideas for a forthcoming issue directly, my mind often balks. If I search to one side or another, ideas inevitably pop up. The peripheral mind is often more creative than its direct cousin. After I draft the initial text, I re-read it at least three different times. Microsoft Word reviews spelling and grammar. Then it goes to the Copy Editor who, over a sushi lunch, reads (and often savages) the draft, and returns it to me stained with green wasabi and soy sauce. I give it two more separate readings, catching several more mistakes and improving a few words. These multiple readings, over a period of five days, are the same fresh views that help solve crossword puzzles and other problems.

Frequent pauses and breaks in the action, combined with the application of different perspectives, sometimes peripheral, can add real value to your risk management process. Risk scenarios and their responses will benefit, refreshed by multiple intuitive and experiential insights. Take time to solve your puzzles. Try to sight the future using oblique views.

Changing Course
(February 2003)

That still, small voice of my cynical alter ego comments to me: "You spend all your time recommending in-depth risk analyses, carefully weighing probabilities, consequences and what other will think. Most of this work is based on history, experience and information collected about past events. Isn't this akin to that joke about the actuary who sits in the back seat of a car, looking through the rear window, advising the driver where to go? Is it realistic to change course using only past data?"

I thought about this for some time before I realized that the problem is closely analogous to rowing a single scull. This is one of my favorite pastimes whenever the waters of Hamburg Cove, in Connecticut, and Long Cove, in Maine, are not covered by ice and are reasonably warm. In my single, a singularly unstable narrow platform, 26 feet long and about 8 inches wide, I wield two ten-foot oars, sit on a sliding seat, and attempt to propel myself backwards into the future. Aren't collisions inevitable?

Experienced scullers glance to port and starboard every few strokes, using their peripheral vision to judge what lies ahead. Some even resort to mounting a tiny mirror on their caps to help see the course. So it is entirely possible to proceed backwards into the future without mishap.

But what happens when an external force, expected or unexpected, creates a problem for the rower? We learn to anticipate the consequences. Where I row along the coast of Maine on early mornings, a close-passing lobster-boat throws a turbulent wake. Since they are working and I'm relaxing, I don't begrudge them their speed. Experience teaches me to turn my bow toward the waves, often stopping until they pass under my hull. At one end of my regular row I also face a strong tidal current running 90 degrees to my course, one that can sweep me 500 feet up or downstream. I alter my course to compensate for the current. In a large ship this is done mathematically, using vector diagrams. In a single scull, I use my eye. On first entering the current, I pick out a lobster-buoy astern and line it up with some landmark further away, a rock, tree or edge of a house. (Avoid using a seagull or blue heron standing on the shore!) I adjust my course keeping those marks aligned, pulling harder on one oar or the other to maintain my bearing. To the landsman I appear to be moving crabwise, but my realized course is straight.

This is a perfect analogy for risk managers. Recognize that we all proceed into the future almost blindly, very much like the actuary. Watch where you come from, but occasionally glance ahead. Peripheral and intuitive vision is important. Pausing for turbulence is perfectly acceptable. And continue to adjust your course for actual and anticipated events. Small, incremental course changes are far better than large, abrupt ones. This will bring you safely to your destination.

Reading the Stanley Cup
(June 2002)

All winter and spring the new books on risk management pile up, causing my wife to issue an ultimatum: read them or out they go! So it's book review time, yet my evenings are spoken for. Yes, it's Stanley Cup playoff time again. To my non-North American readers, the Stanley Cup playoffs are for ice hockey fans what the World Cup is for football (soccer) fans, except that this madness is annual, from mid-April through mid-June. The playoff games are shown almost every evening, into the early hours of the morning when teams from the west coast play or when others go into overtime. I acknowledge that it's difficult to focus on the details of weather derivatives, dangerous bacteria, or securitized risk financing alternatives when the Maple Leafs tie up a game in the last seven seconds and push it into overtime. But here we go!

(1) ***Overkill,*** by Dr. Kimberly M. Thompson, of the Harvard School of Public Health, published by Rodale, Inc., 2002, is a simplified introduction to the perils of bacteria and our over-dependence on antibiotics, the so-called "miracle" drugs we use to correct the slightest illness. Addicted to these drugs, we allow ever-inventive bacteria to become drug-resistant. The new antibiotic-resistant strains of tuberculosis threaten us with the next global pandemic. (*Koivu scores for Montreal: where do they find these fleet Finns?*) Dr. Thompson describes the problem, poses fifty questions to determine a personal "risk quotient," and goes on to suggest alternative means of treating many common illnesses, from abscesses to tooth decay. She follows with further practical recommendations for hygiene in the home and in food storage, preparation, and cooking. Her conclusion: we are entering a new "age of risk management" in which each of us takes greater personal responsibility for crisis resolution. "We need to move beyond the false belief that killing all germs is desirable or even possible. We need to reduce our dependence on antibiotics and antibacterial products and use them only when they're appropriate." Germs, like risks, can be both good and bad. Her book is an excellent primer on personal risk management.

　　(*Ouch, there's Darcy Tucker of the Leafs crumpled into the boards, and Daniel Alfredsson, who hit him, then scores the winning goal!*)

(2) What better book to read during clashes among such teams as the Hurricanes, Avalanche, Thrashers, Devils, Flames, Sharks, and Red Wings than the newest summary on ***Weather Risk Management,***

written by members of the staff of Element Re, an XL Capital division in Stamford, Connecticut, USA. Edited by Eric Banks, Element Re's Chief Risk Officer, this is a detailed analysis of the fundamental nature and economics of weather, the players in the weather market game, from energy companies and insurers to banks and brokers, and the wide variety of developing financial products and strategies. It concerns not only the potential for catastrophes (*Oops, the Hurricanes just blew the Maple Leafs away in overtime, a risk hardly fundable by a derivative*) but also the mundane interests of utilities and oil companies in financing departures from expected counts of heating and cooling degree-days. As the authors proceed into derivatives and insurance-related products and capital market structures, adding pricing theories, portfolio effects, the difficulties of data, legal/regulatory limitations, arcane accounting, and tax treatments, the math becomes more daunting, but the writing remains clear. I begin to see, however, why no one understood what Enron was actually doing! All in all, this is the most thorough review that I've seen of this growing world market. Published by Palgrave (Basingstoke, Hampshire, United Kingdom and New York), 2002. For more information, also go to the Weather Risk Management Association's website—www.wrma.com.

(*Now there's a play: Peter Forsberg, like an opportunistic football player, re-directs the puck off his skate past a sprawled Dominic Hasek, but the kicked goal is disallowed!*)

(3) Christopher Culp, the Managing Director of CP Risk Management and an Adjunct Professor of Finance at the University of Chicago, is the author of an imposing new volume, **The ART of Risk Management**, a discussion of alternative risk transfer, capital structure and the convergence of insurance and capital markets. Published by John Wiley & Sons, Inc, New York earlier this year, this is a thorough and detailed review of many of the new forms of risk financing that challenge corporate financial officers. While I continue to disagree that anything such as "risk transfer" exists (all risk financing is, in effect, risk sharing), Culp's comprehensive analysis commands attention. He begins from the Basel

Committee's vantage point—the quest for setting an optimal capital structure for an organization—and moves to the application of risk management ideas, drawing heavily from his 2001 book, *The Risk Management Process: Business Strategy and Tactics,* also published by Wiley. He describes conventional "risk transformation" products, such as credit, derivatives, insurance and reinsurance. (*An own goal! Patrick Roy of Colorado just had a shot rebound from the back—boards and ricochet off his skate into the Avalanche goal. Mortification!*) Culp concludes with his analysis of the newer risk financing approaches, from captive, self-insurance, finite risk and multi-trigger products to committed capital and the recent range of securitizations. The book also includes several case studies written by guest authors. *The ART of Risk Management* summarizes the growing interaction of traditional insurance, credit and investment banking, suggesting an inevitable melding of approaches that were once firmly separate. It's an imposing reading task, at almost 600 pages, but worth the effort.

(*Another overtime game, won by Chris Drury's delicate pass into the Detroit goal, past Hasek.*)

Time to conclude my reading and slip into bed. It reminds me of the thoughtful words of that good vicar, the Rev. Sydney Smith, who wrote, "I never read a book before reviewing it; it prejudices a man so!"

Changing the Rules
(March 2002)

Enlightenment comes at the strangest moments. Late last month, mesmerized by the extraordinary quality of the men's ice hockey in this year's Winter Olympics, I indulged in the ultimate fantasy of an aging hockey player. I watched four games in succession in one day, eight plus hours of puck!

I first picked up a stick and puck in November 1947. I carved my initials in the puck, marked my stick, and proceeded to a lengthy but hardly illustrious career batting a seamless rubber sandwich along the ice and perfecting a slap shot that was (and remains) a perfect parabola. Fifty-five years have elapsed since that fateful moment and I've played this strange and enticing game every winter (and a few summers, as well) except for two, when I served on a refrigerator ship for the U.S. Navy. We had ice but no rink.

Back to the Olympics: twelve periods of checks, shots and scores, supported by lunch, dinner and an incredulous wife, produced a euphoria not unlike the satori that marks Zen enlightenment! I realized that the human animal makes changes not only after misfortunes occur but also after successful events. More commonly, we are pushed to change after being banged badly by some disaster. But good fortune can also induce transformation. Risk managers use adverse events to provoke new habits. They should learn to use favorable events as well. I offer three current examples, two from this year's Winter Olympics.

The first is Enron, the Houston hot-air balloon that abruptly spewed its innards all over the United States. As historians remind us, it happened before and will happen again. Enron will stimulate needed changes to restore our confidence in financial reports, auditors, securities analysts, bankers and government regulators. Take the auditors. Changes are underway. Auditing and consulting will be separate. I can hear the Accenture partners breathing an enormous sigh of relief following their acrimonious split from Arthur Andersen two years ago. They thought they had lost an important brand name—Andersen Consulting—but they dodged the bullet! Accounting firms will no longer serve as both external and internal auditors. And publicly owned firms may be required to shift their audit relationships every five years. Accounting becomes a radically altered profession but one that may be able to restore its credibility. In this instance, bad news breeds change.

Now consider the figure skating brouhaha in this year's Winter Olympics. After the public outcry (whether warranted or not) on the pair's competition, the skating powers awarded an extra set of gold medals and suggested a radical revision in the method of scoring. They propose fourteen judges instead of nine, with nine scores randomly selected by computer. They will use a new scale of 10 instead of 6: a "perfect 10" will have a new meaning! All of this is to eliminate a public perception of conflict of interest. Here's another example of adversity bringing change.

Finally, I return to men's ice hockey. Here the stimulus for change is not a fiasco but a remarkable success. Huge audiences watched an international game played on a larger ice surface, allowing more speed and passing, in contrast to the cramped National Hockey League rinks that encourage grabbing and holding, slowing the game. The red line is not enforced, allowing longer passes and breakaways. Face-offs take place within 15 seconds, as compared to the 30 to 60 seconds required in North America. There are no two-minute commercial breaks: sponsors must sell their wares, if at all, in short 15 second slots or between periods. Games move more quickly and conclude in two hours instead of almost three. The boards carry no garish advertisements. And best of all, a fight calls for a five minute major misconduct penalty and expulsion from that game and the next. Aha! No more fights! No hulking and often inept "enforcers" played on any of the Olympic teams. So what viewers saw were exceptional displays of hockey skills by the best in the world, and they realized the true excitement of this game. Now will the players, managers and owners in the National Hockey League wake up to the Olympic success and adopt changes that can revitalize this sport? Will this success breed change?

It's time to change the rules in hockey, figure skating and accounting!

Rowing and Risk Management
(August 2000)

A metaphor is a useful tool in building understanding of a difficult idea. Several years ago, I tried relating the discipline of risk management to the art of varnishing, a summer trade that I ply for my menagerie of watercraft. Now it is rowing and risk management.

This summer I found myself again at the Craftsbury Sculling Center for a week's application to the finer points of propelling a single scull through the water quickly and safely. Craftsbury is an ascetic setting in the Northeast Kingdom of Vermont, just beneath the Canadian border. No radio, no television, no newspapers (other than one copy of the Burlington daily). Cell phones don't work and only two pay phones give access to the outside world. We row and eat (well and mightily, I add) three times a day, read and sleep. The focus on rowing is worthy of a monastery.

While skimming the waters of Lake Hosmer, concentrating on the incessant advice of coaches trying to rid me of 50+ years of accumulated bad habits, I reasoned that the sculling process is analogous to our favorite discipline. The rowing motion involves all parts of the body, in a continuous, circular effort of catching the water with the oars, driving them through the water, releasing the blades and recovering for the next stroke. As one coach says, "sculling is an art form—beautiful, graceful, powerful, rhythmic and speedy." So too is risk management an art form—not a science—that requires complete concentration, yet at the same time an almost ethereal relaxation and mystical separation from the effort.

Risk management, like rowing, is a circular, repetitive process. Both require flexibility to respond to changing conditions: wind, waves, current, mental attitude, competition. Both require balance: seeking a blend of reward and punishment to master the current conditions. In sculling, I drive a 28-foot long, pencil-thin shaft of carbonfiber, something that is inherently unstable at rest, through the water to give it both progress and stability. Any organization is inherently unstable at rest: it requires successive decisions, all involving risk, to propel it into progress and change. Risk gives the organization meaning, motion and balance—the keys to its journey.

Scullers and risk managers are similar in one final way: both sit looking backwards, trying to figure out where they are going!

Concentration on all the parts of the process eventually leads to a fusion that enables the sculler and risk manager to transcend the individual parts and reach a point where it becomes almost effortless, where the process is fully integrated into the culture. Over-focus on one step or another, and integration slips away.

One morning at Craftsbury I went out earlier than the others to savor the quiet and the solitary calm of the Lake. At the far end I stopped, turned and paused on my oars. A blue heron stood on a log at the water's edge, staring at me intently, having critiqued my rowing skill. He then turned and lifted effortlessly into the air, as if to disparage my puny attempts at integrated motion. We keep trying!

> *The coach and student ought to consider all aspects of modern scientific training. They should have an understanding of basic rigging, biomechanics, anatomy and physiology . . . The sculler ought to have a keen sense of sculling history and tradition . . . Besides this historical and educational perspective, the sculler can achieve a poetic sense of his own role in this tradition. It is this perspective that helps provide some insight into both the ecology of our natures and one's external environment.*

James C. Joy, *The Art of Sculling*, in paper Dec. 8, 1978

The Captain Speaking
(May 1997)

One of the traditions of the sea is the captain's authority of command and full and absolute responsibility for whatever perils occur. Risk managers should periodically remind their CEOs of this tradition and its application to other organizations. Accepting responsibility is one of the requirements of leadership. Passing the buck is not permissible. Saying that "mistakes were made" is a cop-out. The proper response is "I made a mistake and I will correct it."

Roger Duncan's eloquent editorial in *The Working Waterfront*, for March 1997, reinforces this idea. Commenting on the effect of the plethora of marine safety laws and regulations, Duncan writes "in spite of all these beneficent laws and regulations, the government is not and cannot be responsible for the safety of crews and passengers. It is the skipper's responsibility and his alone. No government can legislate common sense, good judgment and a dash of luck . . . (The skipper) cannot rely on that providence which seems to watch over the ignorant, the careless and the intoxicated. No required equipment can substitute for the wisdom gained from experience."

The idea of accepting and acknowledging responsibility is, regrettably, absent in too many organizations today. It's an idea that risk managers should restore.

The Five Hole
(March 1997)

Every organization has unique vulnerabilities and is constantly altering its defenses to meet these rapidly changing risks, a bit like an ice hockey goalie, moving from side to side, moving out to cut down the angle for a shooter, leaping high to block shots and then flopping on the ice to protect his net. Sticks, pads, gloves, and even the facemask are tools of the trade. Yet vulnerabilities remain. In hockey, the extreme corners of the net carry the designations "one" through "four." They are the exposed points for scoring. But the most vulnerable point, in the estimation of many coaches and players, is the Five Hole, the triangular gap between the goalie's legs and the ice. Arms and sticks move faster than legs, and, since the goalie generally takes a spread-leg stance for greater balance and quick motion, the Five Hole can give a split-second opening for a scoring shot.

The analogy to risk management is obvious. Competition, Murphy, or "the Gods" seek and find that vulnerable point. Risk managers acknowledge that no measure of risk control will completely eliminate the Five Hole: vulnerability is a constant. The key is to reduce that vulnerability to its minimum and then to have a counter-attack capability than can offset the loss and win the encounter. That's the goal of risk management: prepare prudently for the occasional harmful event and yet take strategic advantage of the larger game for eventual victory.

He shoots! He scores!

Solitaire and Time
(September 1997)

I come from a family in which the Protestant Work Ethic is paramount. Both my father and grandfather were Episcopal preachers whose ministries made them available to their parishioners 24 hours a day, seven days a week, and fifty-two weeks a year. Preachers *always* work on Sundays. I attended schools and joined firms that reinforced this idea: going to the office early and leaving late was considered *de rigueur.* I remember a Thanksgiving Day when several of us ran from home to office to professional typist as we tried to finish a risk management report for Safeway Stores, due in Oakland, California, the following Monday morning (with no FedEx, UPS or priority mail then, only regular mail).

Having lived with this burden my entire life, I was appalled to have my ever-loyal Mac announce to me in August that I had spent one hundred (100) hours playing computer solitaire! One hundred hours of wasted time, in total violation of The Ethic. It started inauspiciously, as any addiction does: while waiting on the phone for some ethereal service representative, I clicked Solitaire and started flipping cards. Then it was something to end a writing day. It grew to a starter ("the hair of the dog") and then a mid-day pick-me-up, and now I'm consumed. I still consider the computer impertinent to remind me of the aggregate time spent on this frivolity.

The worst part of my addiction is that I'm not particularly good at the game. My batting average is .135, something that would expel me immediately from baseball's major leagues—with the exception, perhaps, of the always-laboring Red Sox. It's an abysmal record. In addition, my copy editor and wife, who is also addicted to these games, superciliously sniffed that she was batting .185. Of course, she has learned the tricks of undoing moves and using the "play again" button to redress stupid mistakes. She's totally unethical. My ecclesiastical background doesn't permit me to do such things.

The worst part of this sad record is that I don't feel any guilt. In those 100 hours I could have produced ten issues of *Risk Management Reports,* written five learned articles, or read several important books. But I didn't and I'm not sorry! Time seems to have washed away most of the old ethic. Robertson Davies put my mind at ease when I read his comment on time: "Time is one of the great Hobgoblins of our day. There is really no time except the single, fleeting moment that slips by us like water, and to talk about losing time, or saving time, is often a very dubious argument" (*The Merry Heart,* Viking, New York 1997).

So if this issue is a bit late, it's because I'm trying to raise my average to .185.

Postscript: I'm still consumed by the disease in 2005. I've thrown ethics to the winds and adopted all my wife's wiles, raising my average to .211, but her average is now over .250. I struggle onwards.

"Global Cooling"
(September 1997)

I read much in the press about global warming and its effects on our environment. Drought, storms, and floods are supposed to be increasing, leading to horrendous financial costs. While sharing some thought on both global warming and the move of ice hockey teams southwards, I received from Bruce Kirby, otherwise known for his design of sailing yachts, this email that points to an entirely different scenario. Risk managers, take note!

I have hit upon a significant fact of geothermal physics. The recent abundance of ice hockey rinks south of the border and as far down as Florida and Texas, where there should be virtually no ice at any time, and certainly none at this time of year, has resulted in the phenomenon of "global cooling." In addition, condensation from all this ice ("hice" à la Province de Quebec) has served to plug up those holes in the ozone layer, thus intensifying the reversion to our sadly missed "old fashioned winters." Soon we will be able to dispense with artificial hice; we will be able to play in the streets again, and, if the masses return to the national pastime, we will surely run out of rubber hockey pucks. Then we will revert to the favorite missile of our youth ("ute" à la Province de Quebec), the horse ball, or pomme de rue, which is a chunk of second hand oatmeal, bound together with equine body fluids and distributed abundantly on the streets by the docile beasts that pull the dairy and bakery sleds. They are the original and perfect hockey pucks. They take a uniform bounce, they have good carry-through (momentum) and they will hold together until some insensitive ute slams one into the goal post with a slap shot, at which time the pomme de rue will explode into many pieces, some of which will go into the net causing the red light to go on, and confusing the hell out of everyone present or watching on radio. The goalie will yell "Shit!" the referee will shout, "It's a goal," and the opposing coach

will scream "Horseshit!," to which everyone will agree; so they will give
one point to each team and face off at center hice.

Patience
(August 1996)

Summer brings me back to Maine, its long, lazy days and the never-ending rituals of boat maintenance. One of these is varnishing, the careful application of six or more coats of luminous protection for the brightwork on a sailing sloop and the rubrail and sculls for an 18' rowing boat. Each surface is carefully sanded, first with 80 grit and then 120. Then I wait for some warm, dry weather, not too windy, and begin applying thin coats of the best marine varnish (that's varnish that is identical to regular varnish but costs 50% more because it is called "marine"). Each coat should dry at least 24 hours, before it is lightly sanded with even finer paper and a follow-up coat applied. This entire, almost religious, ritual requires anywhere from seven days (if the weather cooperates) to three weeks, after which I bask in the glow of the newly finished wood.

I first wrote about the varnishing process and its application to risk management in September 1994. The compliments of a neighbor on my efforts this year remind me that the lesson needs reiteration. The critical ingredient, of course, is patience. Varnishing cannot be rushed, nor can the creation of effective risk financing. Too many rush precipitously from one risk financing plan to another, from enforced high deductibles in hard conditions to low when the market is soft, from one provider to another on the strength of annual or triennial bids. Too little time means inadequate bonding, just like too few coats of varnish. It's easily marred and we're disappointed with the result. We then start over, trying something new. Often we rush into new offers without the necessary preliminaries (preparation of the "surface") and fail to consider the patience needed in an enduring relationship (between wood and varnish, between organization and risk financing partner).

I've argued that risk financing is "sharing," not "transfer." Shouldn't these relationships, like varnish on brightwork, be more carefully and patiently built up over a period of years, even decades? The results will be more satisfactory. It's a lesson that summer in Maine teaches.

> *If a man must be obsessed by something, I suppose a boat is as good as anything, perhaps a bit better than most. A small sailing craft is not only beautiful, it is seductive and full of strange promise and the hint of trouble.*
>
> **E. B. White, "The Sea and the Wind that Blows,"**
> ***Oxford Book of the Sea***, Oxford University Press, Oxford 1993

CHAPTER 7

Issues in Risk Management

*E*ach January, I try to write about those issues that, in the ensuing twelve months, may be the most important to those responsible for risk management. Looking back, I find that many of my selections were on target, but I also had notable misses. I worried about the growing bubble in the U.S. stock market in 1998, 1999, and 2000 but was several years too early. Other issues are so generic that they persist from one year to the next. Still, it's fun to be a prognosticator every so often. Here are two illustrative essays on these issues, from 2000 and 2003.

Issues for 2000
(January 2000)

"Another opening, another show," wrote Cole Porter in *Kiss Me Kate*. Here we are opening the 27th volume of *Risk Management Reports* in a year with three naughts. Given luck (and proper risk management), my readers will have avoided any computer unpleasantness and are ready to face other risk issues for the new year.

My 1999 issues sported both hits and misses. I forecast the bursting of the stock bubble in the United States (for the second straight year) and found myself staring again at new market records, wondering why I put my money into Treasury bills. Political and military turmoil also topped the list: no miss here, with impeachment in the United States, Kosovo, India-Pakistan, Iraq, Indonesia and Northern Ireland leaping out of the headlines. Other correct calls riveting our attention were the continuing legal hysteria in the United States—the Y2K problem—the development of AIDS into a huge human disaster in Central Africa, the gambling craze (again in the United States), the movement toward a geriatric society in many developed countries, and the need to re-define risk management. There is a persistency to most of these issues, as you will see.

For 2000, I restrict my issues to **financial institutions** and **trust**, two areas that offer unusual opportunities and pitfalls.

First, worry about financial institutions. We're entering a maelstrom of rapid and tumbling change brought about by the globalization of trade and radical upheavals in regulation. Nowhere is this more apparent than in the United States, where the old rules and regulations are crumbling, leaving insurance companies, depository banks and investment firms scrambling to enter each other's businesses. After 66 years, these institutions may now acquire and be acquired by each other. What is likely to happen?

First, look at the condition of the insurance industry. It is in terrible shape. The property and casualty side has under-priced its product for almost 40 years, leading to the suspicion that the proper name for its employees should be undertakers, not underwriters. This resulted in under-reserving and an over-reliance on both investment income and on an outmoded distribution system (insurance agents and brokers) when other financial services are quickly moving to direct relationships. Its overhead costs are exorbitant—averaging almost 30% of each premium dollar. One securities firm suggests that the industry overspends $54 billion annually in "sloppy and redundant paper processes." Customers rate its services as D-, almost failing: the industry has a chronic inability to deliver a policy on time without mistake, and its treatment of claimants borders on the absurd. Apparently it thinks most claimants, including its own policyholders, are inherently dishonest, and therefore it creates delays and obfuscations that fulfill its prophecy: claimants become so irate that they do, in fact, inflate losses!

Some investment analysts argue that the industry is one-third—or $100 billion—over-capitalized. They press for capital reductions to increase ROI and stock prices. At the same time, other observers warn of the rising susceptibility of insurers to wind, water and earthquake catastrophes, any one of which may sink a number of major carriers. Is it too much or too little?

Consider also the rapidly declining reputation of the industry: public outrage at medical insurers and HMOs, accused of meddling in medicine and substituting profit for sound health care; lawsuits that now forbid insurers from using secondary market instead of OEM (original equipment manufacturer) parts for auto damages; lawsuits that re-define both coverage and exclusions; and the often-comic political machinations of less-than-reputable persons trying to become elected state insurance commissioners.

No wonder Myron Picoult, the astute industry analyst for Wasserstein Perella Securities Inc., writing in *Business Insurance* (September 20, 1999), says "the industry is in a period that is both mesmeric and frightening."

What's likely to happen in 2000? The welcome demise of the Glass-Steagall Act, the extraordinary productivity inherent in new information technology, and the threatened change in accounting rules in the United States, from "pooling-of-interests" to the "purchase" method, suggest twelve months of intense jockeying for position. Banks will be the aggressors. I doubt that they try insurance through the sales route. This sandbags them with underwriting and expense inefficiencies, plus the sad claims-handling reputation of conventional companies. I suspect they will use the next twelve months, before the new accounting rules take effect, to acquire selected property & casualty insurers with knowledgeable underwriters, modest expenses, and reasonable claims-paying reputations. If that fails, they will create underwriting vehicles *de novo*, blending insurance risk financing with existing banking products and services, stealing quality personnel and services from other firms. In a few, very few, cases, insurers may actually acquire banks.

The second effect in 2000 will be the acceleration of direct insurance services to customers, particularly personal and small business buyers. Insurance companies that fail to offer coverage directly may find themselves hopelessly buried with their albatross counterpart, the agency and brokerage system. The President of the Federal Reserve Bank of Dallas summarized the situation in the *Wall Street Journal:* "The real key to our growth in productivity is information technology and the Internet revolution . . . the Internet's disintermediation is squeezing it all down to 'wholetail'." My prediction: within five years, more than 50% of all risk financing will be purchased directly from risk financing institutions.

This, of course, does not mean that there is not a position for "advisors." Some will succeed, but as the consultants to their clients, not as commission-paid salespeople.

I have one final comment about financial institutions in 2000. We have yet to conclude how best to regulate these new combinations. Will it be state/provincial, national, regional or international? In the United States the utility and efficiency of state regulation of insurance is under serious question. With global competition, I believe that some form of "Basel Committee" will be necessary to oversee financial organizations, with all their permutations. Global risk-based capital requirements are inevitable, however much they may impinge on national sovereignty, with the resulting and inevitable chauvinistic political outcry. In the US, a rapid move to Federal regulation will probably occur, especially if some form of the proposed Policyholder Disaster Protection Act (H.R.2749), for catastrophe reserving, is approved.

So we have an extraordinary opportunity to create and deliver new risk financing products, attuned to current and future needs, blending the skills of three financial institutions, banks, investment houses, and insurers. The pitfall is that some will not make it.

My second issue for 2000 is trust. My over-arching concern is the growing lack of trust that individuals have in profit-making corporations and their governmental servants. Some of this disillusionment is evident in the frequency and size of individual and class action lawsuits, many that invoke patently frivolous allegations. We simply can't trust one another.

The noises from Seattle early in December illustrate the magnitude of the problem. Luddites on both sides insinuated the worst possible inclinations of the others, and the anarchists said "to hell" with everything! The World Trade Organization could not see that its deliberations should be far more transparent and reflective of broader issues than simply trade. The demonstrating groups piously intoned their concern for workers and environments in other jurisdictions while attempting to protect their own comfortable and insulated positions. Neither side could believe that the other possessed even a modicum of altruism or honesty. There was no trust.

The Economist (lead editorial, December 11) summarized it neatly: "Free trade, like freedom in general, is not a panacea. It is not likely to bring better welfare on its own. But also, it is not likely simply to enrich multinationals and destroy the planet. Trade is about greater competition, which weakens the power of vested interests. It is about greater opportunity for millions rather than privileges for the few."

When we have elected officials who patently lie to us, when we have an industry deny for years that its products are harmful to our health (in the face of almost uniform scientific evidence to the contrary), when other scientists assure us of the relative safety of some technology in terms that are incomprehensible, trust disappears. And when trust evaporates, so too does civility and confidence in the uncertain future. We turn to constant threats, recriminations, and the use of lawsuits to redress imagined imbalances.

Last year's film, *A Civil Action*, drawn from the earlier book of the same title by Jonathan Harr, illustrates that lack of trust: the plaintiffs mistrusted neighbor corporations and even their own attorney; the corporations mistrusted the community and the civil justice system; the court mistrusted the competing lawyers. Who can we trust if everyone seems hell-bent on personal gain?

How is the public to react when a corporation appears to value its shareholders over any other constituents? A review in the *Journal of Contingencies and Crisis Management* (September 1999) described the first response of the company that owned the *Estonia*, the ship that sank in the Baltic on the night of September 28, 1994 with the loss of 800 lives. The next morning the company advised the press that insurance covered the loss of the ship and possible ensuing damages! No wonder that the public loses trust in corporations, organizations that, in Peter Bernstein's words, give evidence of "a ruthless and cold-blooded drive to maximize shareholder return."

If mutual trust is rapidly disappearing, what can we do about it? Lance Odden, the Headmaster of Connecticut's Taft School, recently wrote in the school's magazine: "None of us can entirely change the world, but we are morally challenged to try to make it a better place." This is as true of the organizational risk manager as it is of a teacher or preacher. Perhaps this new century will see a retreat from the "me" decade of the 1990s toward a new recognition of our interconnectedness with others, our communities, and our environment. Yes, we need to be efficient, and productive, and profitable, but not at the expense of all those values that create a livable community.

We place great stock in "scientific" risk assessment. But how does the public view it? Peter Montague, in an Internet-published essay that John Ross (*The Polar Bear Strategy*) brought to my attention, writes: "Risk assessment is inherently an undemocratic process because most people cannot understand the data, the calculations, or the basis for the risk assessor's judgment." How can we democratize the process without compromising its intellectual rigor?

The solution lies in improving how we communicate with all those affected by our decisions. There's an eye-opening chapter in *Risk and Responsibility,* by William Leiss and Christina Chociolko (McGill-Queen's University Press, 1994), describing a power line siting controversy in British Columbia. In 1989, British Columbia Hydro proposed additions to an existing set of power lines to support a pulp and paper plant expansion. Leiss and Chociolko tell the fascinating story of the public reaction to the plan, the conflicting scientific evidence offered about the risks of electric and magnetic fields, the growing resentment of both sides in the argument, the attempt of government to intervene and arbitrate, and the conclusions, unsatisfactory to all. It's a lesson that every risk manager should read, mark, and inwardly digest. It is a lesson of the erosion of trust and the failure to communicate intelligently and in a timely fashion. It is a lesson of how not to present so-called "expert" scientific data to the public. By the end of the affair, no one participant trusted another.

Another example is the decision by Royal Dutch/Shell to sink its Brent Spar facility in the North Sea. The outcry from environmental organizations, including Greenpeace, eventually forced the company to scrap it ashore, even though most expert opinion, including that of some "greens," was that sinking it was the least offensive to the environment. The lesson: consider seriously the views and risk perceptions of all interested parties before making a decision.

Who can we believe? How can we establish mutual credibility? That is the question that risk managers should ask in 2000 as they attempt to rebuild the bridge of trust that once existed with multiple stakeholders. We must learn how to communicate clearly and intelligently with all of our audiences.

> *The sea, if it teaches nothing else, does at least compel a submission to the inevitable which resembles patience.*
>
> **Patrick O'Brian,** *Blue at the Mizzen,*
> **W. W. Norton & Co., New York 1999**

Issues for 2003
(January 2003)

A gray cloud of hesitancy hangs over all of us. The political euphoria following the fall of Communism and the economic fantasies of the 1990s are distant memories, blown away by present realities, political, economic and environmental. Global politics dominates the horizon. Will war occur in Iraq? If so, what are the possible repercussions throughout the Middle East? Can the Israeli-Palestinian conflict sink any lower, or will the new elections bring forth some sanity? Can India solve its growing internal problems as well as its continuing disagreement with Pakistan? Will the Sri Lanka and Northern Ireland truces hold? Is Indonesia on the road to disintegration? What will the world do with North Korea? How soon before it implodes? Will the political turmoil in Venezuela and Colombia infect the rest of South and Central America? The economic scene is no less worrisome. The United States, the world's largest economy, is awash in personal debt, crippled by inadequate saving, and saddled with an enormous current-account deficit, even as a real estate bubble floats precariously over many parts of the country. Is it out of its recession or heading into a "double-dip?" *The Economist* (September 28, 2002) suggests that "the business cycle is likely to become more volatile again over the coming years" and that the U.S. recession "is far from over." Europe watches anxiously as the U.S. stock market dips and surges, signaling little but uncertainty. In South America, Argentina's economy shrunk more than 10% in 2002, and its difficulties could easily infect Brazil, Uruguay, Paraguay and Bolivia, as well as Colombia and

Venezuela. War and many possible aftershocks in the Middle East could dramatically affect the cost and availability of oil, on which so much of the developed world depends. Japan seems chronically unable to repair its wounded banking system, leaving it mired in continued slump.

And if our political and economic worries were not enough, we are warned again about new environmental woes. Global warming is now an acknowledged fact even though we remain uncertain as to whether we are the cause (the pumping of gases into our atmosphere) or it is some periodic climatic anomaly. The answer is probably both, and that we must prepare for radical weather change. The problem of water is one outgrowth of climate change. Shrinking glaciers in the Andes threaten future water supplies for inhabitants on both sides of the mountains. The water from the Colorado River in the United States, so sub-divided that not a trickle escapes to Mexico, is tied up in continuing litigation over its ownership. In Central Asia, the monumental plan of the Soviet Union to transform desert into plantation by erecting 45 dams and numerous canals on the Syr and Amu Rivers has created a parched morass in which the Aral Sea— at one time the sixth-largest inland lake in the world—has shrunk to a polluted one-third its original size. The *New York Times* (December 9, 2002) calls it a "shrunken, dust-shrouded necklace of brine lakes." Afghanistan and five new countries—Uzbekistan, Turkmenistan, Kazakhstan, Kyrgyzstan and Tajikistan—depend on these waters, now hopelessly mismanaged and wasted. The conflicts over the use of water— for drinking, for farming or for industry—are global problems that promise to provoke increasing violence in the coming years.

And if these ominous warnings are not enough, the National Academy of Sciences in the United States published a startling paper in 2002, "Abrupt Climate Change: Inevitable Surprises." It suggests that our classic supposition that all climate change is slow and incremental could be wrong. Examination of 11,500-year-old ice-cores taken from Greenland shows that rapid changes, within as little as three to ten years, have occurred several times on the past 100,000 years. How would the population of the Earth adjust to a doubling of annual precipitation is just three years? Or to a 14-degree jump in average temperature in ten years? These ice-cores indicate that such explosive changes are possible. This idea of a precipitous climate change, warmer or colder, is not new. Loren Eiseley, an anthropologist at the University of Pennsylvania, wrote in 1970 in *The Invisible Pyramid:*

> "Beginning on some winter night the snow will fall steadily for a thousand years and hush in its falling the spore cities whose seed has flown. The delicate traceries of the frost will slowly dim the glass in the observatories and all will be as it had been before the virus wakened. The long trail of Halley's comet, once more returning, will pass like a ghostly matchflame over the unwatched grave of the cities. This has always been their end, whether in the snow or in the sand."

So can you blame us if we are a bit hesitant at the start of 2003?

This issue summarizes some of my thoughts on global, strategic and tactical risk issues for the next twelve months, just as I've done for the past decade. In January 1999, my concerns were economic instability and the stock market "bubble," plus legal mass hysteria in the U.S. court system, the effect of the computer, gambling, the geriatric society and re-defining risk management. In 2000, they were the continuing "bubble" and the decline of trust in institutions. In 2001, I addressed governance and risk management: how it should be structured, led, coordinated and communicated. Last year my three issues were credibility (again), resilience and perspective.

This year I focus on a wider range of risk management issues within the three areas that sub-divide the discipline: market, operational and public policy risks.

First, market risks. In international currency the U.S. dollar is beginning to fall, as the euro gains strength. Sweden is to vote on adopting the euro and the admission of new members to Europe means a wider spread and perhaps greater stability of the euro in the next few years. Interest rates have nowhere to go but up in the United States, Europe and Japan. Our techniques for hedging and sharing these risks are sophisticated and effective, but, as organizations grow in size and global spread, these techniques may diminish in importance. Yet it is in credit risk that I see the greatest rumblings of discontent. In *Risk Management Reports,* April 2001, I noted the forebodings of Avinash Persaud, a managing director of

State Street Bank, in which he suggested that the proposed Basel 2 accords could lead to an increase in systemic risk for banks if they adopted a herd-like response to the new rules and played follow-the-leader. He elaborated on that thesis in his first Mercer Memorial Lecture at London's Gresham College on October 3, 2002, entitled "The Macroeconomics of Basel."

Persaud suggests "the starting point of good regulation is aligning the points of government intervention with the points of market failure." He then cited three characteristics of banks: they pose systemic risks, they are part of the information industry, and they exhibit herd behavior. He went on: "But the irony is that the accoutrements of sophisticated risk management, daily marking-to-market and market-sensitive risk limits, only provide a defense if a handful of banks use them. If regulators encourage all banks to use them they will provide no defense and will make the financial system as a whole riskier." His conclusion is thus: "Basel 2 will lead to more amplified cycles and more instability. It is complex where it should be simple. It focuses on processes when it should focus on outcomes. And it is implicitly pro-cyclical when it should be explicitly contra-cyclical." For Persaud's full arguments, go to www.gresham.ac.uk/commerce/. He presents a refreshing contrarian view.

So much for systemic credit risk. What about the reliability of individual financial institutions? Persaud also raises intriguing questions about the security of many insurance and reinsurance companies, especially those in Europe, that have aggressively added global credit derivatives to their balance sheets. In his second Gresham College lecture, on November 14, 2002, Persaud asked, "Where have all the credit risks gone?" He noted that non-performing loans are at an all-time high of almost $900 billion, having increased by 20% in 2002 alone, yet bank balance sheets continue to look healthy. Why? He attributes this anomaly to the increased use of credit derivatives, with a ten-fold increase to $2 *trillion* in only five years. "Financial innovation has enabled risks to be sliced and diced," he says, leading to better matching and spreading. But many of these financial instruments went to insurance companies as they sought higher yields than government bonds and non-existent underwriting profits. As Persaud noted, "Whenever financial institutions go after yield as a group, regulators should sit up!" The insurers and reinsurers, in turn, hedged the "toxic slice" of credit swaps into the secondary bond and equity markets, the very markets that are currently so volatile. He concluded that the "folly of what insurance companies have been up to" is the "reckless pursuit of yield." He continued, "banks have shifted credit risks to insurance companies, which have hedged themselves by going short the equity markets, which has significantly added to their volatility." And he warned that, "in today's fluid financial markets, the spread of risks has less to do with exactly who owns the risk, and more to do with how risks are treated. The more risks are valued, traded and hedged *in the same way* (my italics), in the same markets, the greater are systemic risks." So both Basel and credit swaps create greater, not less, systemic risk.

Next, consider operational risks. Many of these risks fall into the arena of insurance underwriting, the same industry that Persaud faulted in its handling of credit risks. So another major issue for 2003 is the financial integrity of the non-life business, especially North America and Europe. Despite radical, and some say unconscionable, rate increases post-September 11, 2001, most of the increased revenue went to reinforce inadequate reserves. The overall financial capacity of the non-life business to underwrite risk dropped by almost 25% in 2002, according to the U.S.-based Insurance Information Institute (from $920 billion to $690 billion). This occurred despite the addition of new capital by entrepreneurs taking advantage of the higher rates. The anguished plea by insurance CEOs in the United States for government reinsurance for future terrorism was answered and now these same insurers, many of which cancelled terrorism coverage, must actually underwrite the risk, something they seem latently incapable of doing, despite the government's excess largesse. The Hart-Rudman Report, in October 2002, warned that the United States remains vulnerable to and unprepared for further acts of terrorism. Given the deteriorating global situation, insurers and their reinsurers must expect a higher frequency of terrorist acts. While the individual severity of these acts may not be as terrible as September 11, their aggregate cost could easily exceed the overall industry deductibles that start at $10.5 billion and end at $22.5 billion in the third year. And note that the U.S. government reinsurance will lapse after three years! Add to this gloomy assessment the mounting claims from past uses of asbestos. The Rand Institute for

Civil Justice reported more than $54 billion already spent on asbestos lawsuits, a total that may mount to as much as $260 billion by 2050. Much of this loss will hit the non-life insurance business, even if the U.S. Congress passes some legislation to limit liability. The primary issue in operational risk must be the security of financial counterparties. The non-life industry, especially in the United States, doesn't look any stronger for its upswing in premiums.

The third area of risk is public policy. The global risks mentioned earlier, such as climate change and our shrinking water supply—plus population growth, aging and the pandemic of AIDS—are government concerns that inevitably affect all corporations and organizations. I see two interesting strategic issues for risk managers in 2003. The first is how individual corporations respond to environmental problems. Corporations like BP have decided to take a constructive and pro-active approach to their pollution by setting—and meeting—their own reduction goals. If the United States and some other governments won't respond to Kyoto, then some corporations will and, in so doing, will earn credit from the public. Like-minded companies now also trade pollution credits on the Chicago Exchange, a process that proves to be effective in creating overall reductions. These are areas where risk managers can demonstrate that an early and creative response to environmental degradation results in the opportunity of differentiation from the pack and favorable publicity with stakeholders. After all, the basic goal of risk management is building and maintaining confidence with these groups.

The second issue is the on-going debate about the application of excessive caution concerning new services and goods, such as pharmaceuticals, chemicals and bio-engineered products. The so-called "Precautionary Principle," which states that we should err on the side of caution at all times, is under serious discussion when it appears to limit or restrain needed innovation. Here again, corporate risk managers can inform themselves on the debate and suggest that leaders of their organizations participate. Excessive precaution may cripple incentives and new applications. The discipline of risk management will help demonstrate the proper balance between possible benefits and potential harms. The current discussion in the United States over renewed smallpox vaccinations is a case in point.

I raised the issue of trust in January 2000 and repeated it in January 2002, especially in the context of public policy. It is still paramount. Political and profit-making organizations alike must re-establish and then maintain organizational credibility with stakeholders. Organizational governance is now the focal issue in both Europe and North America, and risk management, on an enterprise-wide basis, is one response contributing to improvement. New rules and regulations (like the Sarbanes-Oxley Law in the United States), new "standards" (like the 2002 U.K. Standard issued by the Institute of Risk Management), and lists of "best practices" will help—but not solve—the underlying problem: changing the organizational culture. That must be the continuous goal of the risk management practice.

These market, operational and public policy risk issues are opportunities for the risk management discipline to dispel the fog of hesitancy that inhibits our decision-making. Our discipline gives managers the tools to cast light on uncertainty, delineating risks in terms of their probable likelihood and consequences. Risk management enables us to make better decisions.

We have a full plate of challenging issues for 2003, just as we now have a menu of tools to dissipate that demoralizing gray cloud of hesitancy. I'd like to think that I see a shaft of sunlight breaking through this gloom. I'm always the optimist. As William Safire of *The New York Times* wrote in early December, now is the time to "launch the war on uncertainty." *That* could well be the risk managers' mantra for 2003.

> *The media will be bulging with economists' forecasts of business, stocks, bonds, and the kitchen sink in 2003. Read these predictions with care. Better yet, skip them and read something useful like the book reviews or the jokes column.*
>
> **Peter Bernstein, *Economics and Portfolio Strategy*,**
> **December 15, 2002**

CHAPTER 8

Risk Communication

*T*oo many of us sit sequestered in our castles, surrounded by sycophants who speak our increasingly stilted language. We understand each other, but outsiders cannot comprehend our Babel of sound. That's perhaps the most critical problem of risk management in the early 21st century—our inability to communicate with others outside our sub-disciplines. For some years now, I've tried to stimulate a greater two-way dialogue among these sub-disciplines plus a clearer and continuing dialogue with the public.

A New Language of Risk
(January 1995)

In November of 1994, I gave two speeches, one in London and the other in New York, that were widely reported in the trade press. I offered a skeptical, contrarian view of both the insurance industry and risk managers, arguing that both had failed those they serve. The insurance industry balks at risk, is inherently unstable, is poorly managed, and, in part as a result of these inadequacies, is losing to its financial competition—banks and government. Risk managers, in turn, over-focus on insurance, have missed service opportunities, and are married to their vendors. I readily plead guilty to using hyperbole in challenging the inadequacies of the present, but I went on to define some needs of the future and seven positive tools that both insurers and risk managers could employ to fulfill their responsibilities. They are:

- A new language of risk
- Tailored financial instruments
- Tailored services
- Direct access to financial institutions
- Reduction of non-essential costs
- Long-term partnerships
- Linkage with society

Risk, which I define as "the compound estimate of the probable frequency, probable severity and public perception of harm," is a confusing concept. According to Morningstar, commenting in the January 1995 issue of the *Fidelity Independent Investor*, "risk is beginning to muscle its way to the foreground—where it belongs . . . There's just too much evidence supporting the point that risk, not return, should be what investors consider first." Yet risk remains a "fuzzier concept" (Morningstar's words) than "return." Organizations have different and often conflicting measures of risk, with little consistency or correlation. One set may apply to the market and financial instruments, another to natural hazards, and still a third to toxic chemicals and other pollutants. Some are quantitative, others highly intuitive.

For example, "market" risk is measured by such abstract terms as "beta" (volatility relative to a market index), "delta" (changes in values as compared to other instruments), "gamma" (the effect of non-linear price changes on the behavior of the portfolio), "vega" (the change in the behavior of the portfolio arising from changes in the implied volatility of the underlying instruments), and "theta" (the change in the behavior of the portfolio arising from the passage of time). Confused? You should be! These definitions are from an August 1993 paper by Charles Sanford, Chairman of Bankers Trust. I highly recommend this paper, despite these arcane references, as it describes the possible evolution of financial institutions in the next 25 years. It also illustrates the risk communication problems we face.

In his paper, Sanford defines the functions of a financial institution— such as a commercial bank, investment bank, or insurance company—as "financing, risk management, trading and positioning, advising, and transaction processing." The "key to the system," in his view, will be development of "wealth accounts" that incorporate both liquid and illiquid assets and liabilities, allowing the availability of "instant credit" secured by these accounts. Drawing on the shift from Newtonian physics to quantum physics, Sanford foresees a comparable shift to "particle finance" that incorporates the work of chaos theorists and "fuzzy logic." It will uncover all of the risk variables in operations and financing and lead to "the most efficient balance of risk and return."

In the area of chemicals, pharmaceuticals, and similar products, many organizations use sophisticated models of probabilistic risk assessment in order to make decisions on the manufacture, use, and ultimate disposal of products. These models are also used by regulators in deciding how safe is "safe enough." Much of the methodology, however, is based on extrapolations from animal tests, since tests on humans are less possible, and on the assumptions of "experts," all of which can be flawed. Management waits in a quandary, not knowing whether its efforts have been sufficient, or overzealous.

Some sanity may be creeping into risk analyses and economic responses. In December 1994, General Motors and the U.S. Department of Transportation announced an agreement on the recall of some six million GM pickup trucks with sidesaddle gasoline tanks mounted outside the truck frame. Since these vehicles are susceptible to fire when struck from the side in higher speed situations, a recall was proposed. GM and the government decided to forego the recall, which might have cost GM over $1 billion, for a GM payment of $51.3 million to support other Federal safety programs. It was a matter of risk analysis. The recall arguably could have saved 32 lives resulting from future collision/fires, but the expenditure of the $51.3 million in a variety of programs is projected to save *at least* 50 lives and prevent 6,000 injuries. Is this a reasonable trade-off? It seems so, and it was based on risk assessment. Yet can a manufacturer make design and cost decisions today, relying on regulatory and judicial reason in the future?

In the natural hazard and property arena we conventionally measure risk with such tools as "MFL" (Maximum Foreseeable Loss), drawing on engineering estimates. In liability and workers' compensation, large databases allow actuaries to trend and develop the past into various projections with different confidence levels for frequency and severity variability. Actuaries can also use Monte Carlo simulations where data are inadequate. We can use Delphi processes and other qualitative risk estimates (see Vernon Grose's *Managing Risk: Systematic Loss Prevention for Executives* and Peter Schwartz's *The Art of the Long View*).

Our problem is that these risk assessments remain uncoordinated and unconnected, leaving senior decision-makers with a confused assortment of numbers and analyses. We need *a new language of risk* to consolidate the wide variety of techniques now in use. This language will measure both *volatility* (the deviation from annual and multi-year expected frequency, severity, and aggregation) and *correlation* (how various risks and their responses affect one another: are they additive, subtractive, or does a multiplier effect occur?) In this way we can aggregate "risk" as a function of both "equity" and "return."

Several organizations are moving toward a combined view of risk. "RiskMetrics," a copyrighted computer methodology for estimating total market risk, was developed by New York's J. P. Morgan & Co. Inc. Available to bank customers and subscribers, "RiskMetrics" applies "consistently calculated volatilities and correlation forecasts" in estimating market risk, based on a "Value-at-Risk approach." Morgan calls its system a "high-quality toolkit," emphasizing that "no amount of sophisticated analytics will replace experience and professional judgment in managing risks." Its goal is to give senior managers a *daily* measure of credit, operational, liquidity, and market risks.

I suspect that this nascent technology will, in time, expand to cover all types of risks faced by any organization. Rather than annual risk reviews (less frequently for many), all risks will be consolidated daily: financial/market, political/regulatory, legal liability and operational. Is this impractical? I don't think so. Technology and a new appreciation of risk make it possible. One of the obvious benefits will be the ability to focus controls on those risks with the highest potential effect and to develop a more broadly based financing response—taking advantage of internal resources, bank lines of credit, investor funds, derivatives, and conventional insurance and reinsurance.

Finally, no one individual within an organization is capable of developing this "new language of risk." It will require a multi-disciplined effort of numerous skills and it will take a number of years to accomplish.

I believe that it will happen and that it represents opportunity for the far-sighted risk manager.

Listening and Telling
(June 2000)

Fourteen years ago, in the May-June 1986 issue of *Risk Management Reports*, I published a portion of a paper by Vincent Covello, Detlof von Winterfeldt, and Paul Slovic on communicating information about health, society and environmental risks. The authors confirmed "risk communication is one of the most important tasks facing risk managers today." Their analysis of communication difficulties included four basic issues: (1) *message problems*: information obscured in technical jargon, (2) *source problems*: lack of trust in those reporting information, (3) *channel problems*: issues such as media bias, poor timing, oversimplification, inaccuracies and distortions, and (4) *receiver problems*: strong beliefs, perceptions, lack of interest and a reluctance to make or accept trade-offs.

These problems remain with us. Science, technology, and economics remain at odds with public comprehension. Risk itself is misconstrued, as many fail to see or deliberately disregard its reward side. We still slip into incomprehensible jargon at the slightest provocation, further eroding any trust that might exist. I described "trust" as one of the two major risk management issues for 2000, and five recent papers and developments endorse that selection.

First, the co-founders of the Global Association of Risk Professionals, Lev Borodovsky and Marc Lore, writing in *Risk Professional* (November 1999), confirm that "no matter what types of methods are used, the key to risk management is delivering risk information in a timely and succinct fashion, while ensuring that key decision makers have the time, the tools, and the incentive to act upon it." The right information presented to the right people at the right time is the goal of communication. Our challenges are how this information is phrased and distributed, in what form, and to whom.

Second, "How do we eliminate the risk of suffocating under the heap of communication trash?" asks the *Magazine 2000* of the Bavarian

Reinsurance Company, in a special issue devoted to Communication. It's a critical question, given the explosion of information available on the Internet. The authors of twenty-one "examples" in this issue confirm that, even as we try to enlighten others about what we know, we inadvertently create misunderstanding. The graphics, prose and photographs of this publication challenge the eye, the intellect, and the imagination. The essays explore such topics as choice, image, language, abbreviation, wishful thinking, certainty, fakery, sign language, simplification, violence, advertising, secrets, perception, buzzwords, attention-span, and, perhaps most importantly, silence.

For example, Michael Rutschky asks, "What is it that makes silence so mighty? One person's silence generates a kind of vacuum that unerringly sucks the speech out of others so as to fill the void." That reminds me of a lesson that my father learned. A long-time Episcopal minister, he contracted cancer of the larynx in his late fifties and had his vocal cords removed. He learned esophageal speech so that he would not become a preacher who could not preach and a pastor who could not talk with his parishioners, but the new speech form was slower and more difficult for him. He found, however, that greater silence necessitated by his surgery forced him to listen more, something that he was convinced made him a better minister. His "silence" elicited speech and became its own parishioner therapy.

Rutschky's essay on abbreviation also makes the point that what is unsaid—what is inferred—may be more important than what appears in print. "Are we not confronted with messages whose invisible and subliminal resonance is still more important than what is said in black and white?" It may be more useful to leave some matters to the imagination.

The Japanese illustrate this point in their classic poetry form, the seventeen syllable haiku. A few words can stimulate ideas and visions in the imagination. Take, for example, one haiku from Sôkan, as translated into an English couplet by Harold Stewart (*A Network of Fireflies,* Charles E. Tuttle Co., Rutland, VT 1960):

> That flight of egrets, if they gave no cry,
> Would be a streak of snow across the sky.

Third, public relations experts are specialists in modern communication, and I turned to my good friend Marion Pinsdorf, at Fordham University, for her insights on this subject. I've already published two of her papers, "How Hype and Glory Gull," on the "conspiracy of denial" prevalent in the contingency planning of many organizations (*RMR* Jan/Feb 1993) and "Supplying Your Own Banana Peels," on the hubris and arrogance that exacerbate crisis situations (*RMR* Nov/Dec 1993). She promptly sent me a paper that she delivered to a symposium of the Institute of Public Relations in April this year. It confirmed the importance of listening to *all* stakeholders, not just those who hold the largest blocks of stock, and of the self-deception inherent in an over-reliance on numbers. An avid student of military history, she used the examples of the General George McClellan and Robert McNamara to illustrate her point. McClellan, a Union leader during the Civil War, accepted notoriously inflated numerical estimates of Confederate strength to avoid engaging the enemy. McNamara, the US Secretary of Defense during the Vietnam War, conversely relied on inaccurate and equally inflated statistics to perpetuate a losing situation. Both demonstrate that numbers can mislead when not counterbalanced with intuition and judgment.

Fourth, many of these ideas and perceptions have been brought together in a new monograph written by Karen Thiessen and published by the Conference Board of Canada. "Don't Gamble with Goodwill: The Value of Effectively Communicating Risks," (*CBC Report 284-00*, March 2000) is a brief, thorough synopsis of current risk communication thinking. It relies heavily on the work of Vincent Covello, cited above. To Thiessen, "Communicating risks is the process of sharing information about an actual or perceived risk in an open and frank manner. It is essential to building trust with your audience, be it the community, public, employees, shareholders, or other stakeholders." She describes a program that delivers the right information at the right time to the right people. She recommends that a strong and trained communication team be a part of any risk management structure, a team versed in the Seven Cardinal Rules of Risk Communication (from the Covello Group):

- Accept and involve the public as a legitimate partner.
- Plan carefully and evaluate performance.

- Listen to your audience.
- Be honest, frank, and open.
- Coordinate and collaborate with other credible sources.
- Meet the needs of the media.
- Speak clearly, with compassion.

To what extent do the media contribute to continuing misunderstandings of risk? They naturally over-focus on the negative, as bad news generates more attention than good. Our attention is riveted to the news reports of the one child who dies from a vaccine shot, as we disregard the hundreds of thousands spared from disease and death. We cannot and should not try and subvert the media, but over the years building bridges of mutual respect and support with key individuals in the media can mean a more reasoned response when your name hits the press. Writers and reporters are people, after all, to whom the same rules of communication apply.

Fifth, the Society for Risk Analysis has just formed a new discussion group on risk communication. "Risk-com" is a listserv, an un-moderated public discussion forum on the Internet designed to promote communication among those interested in this growing field. I hope that risk managers from the operational and financial risk arenas will join the safety, health, and environmental representatives sponsoring this group. To subscribe, send an email message to risk-com-request@umich.edu.

Fourteen years on, we are still learning how to advise our multiple publics and "investor" groups about what we know and don't know about risk. Communication is a continuous process of informing people about rewards and penalties. It remains the most critical and most under-addressed element of risk management.

> ... there is a public that extends far beyond a company's customers, partners, employees, shareholders, and stakeholders, and which is inclined to judge a company and its business partners according to moral criteria.
>
> **Dirk Baecker, "Receivers," in *Communication*,**
> **Bavarian Reinsurance Company, Munich 2000**

Risk Communication Again
(October 2000)

Is it important to involve our stakeholders in the process of assessing and responding to risk as we make decisions? I've already urged that this become a key part of the process. Others disagree. A diametrically opposed comment came from Jack Dowie, in an article in issue 2-2000 of *Risk Management: An International Journal:* "Better risk communication has no role to play in improved decision making." That bald assertion forced me to review my own position.

Dowie's point, as I read him, is that "decision analysis involves raising the analysis-to-intuition ratio in judgment and decision-making significantly above that which characterizes every-day politico-scientific, professional and lay discourses." Since "most people's judgment and decision-making" are corrupted by biases, preconceptions, and flawed analyses, bringing them into the equation means, too often, "that 'risk' [is] being used strategically, consciously or unconsciously, to *prevent* (my emphasis) discussion and debate being raised to the higher ratio that transparency requires, while giving the impression that it was becoming more 'scientific'."

I acknowledge his point. He seeks a higher and purer approach to decisions. Listening to many other voices easily distorts and delays decisions, but since these very decisions affect many others, don't we have a responsibility to bring them into the process, however messy it may become? Can we really stand above the throng, like all-knowing seers? Democracy is not always efficient, but it is the best system yet devised.

Luckily I found some support for my position in four recent publications. The first is from academia. John Shortreed, head of the Institute for Risk Research, at the University of Waterloo, in Canada, who prepared with two associates, L. Craig and S. McColl, a "Draft Benchmark Framework for Risk Management," for NERAM, the Network for Environmental Risk Assessment and Management. In it the authors summarize the "guiding principles" for our discipline, drawn from Australian, New Zealand, Canadian and U.S. sources. One of those principles is: "explicit consideration of stakeholder views of the acceptability of the risk management options through *early and ongoing involvement* (my emphasis) in the decision process." They then describe the strategic, tactical and operational risks that face all decision-makers, suggesting that one of the key goals in building and maintaining the "trust of stakeholders" is their "acceptance of operations, programs, decision, and analyses," their "satisfaction with risk communication efforts," and "their acceptance of residual risk."

They call for a continuing "two-way dialogue" with stakeholders: "The organization should have a process in place for identifying, communicating and consulting with stakeholders. Stakeholders can include decision-makers, individuals who are or who perceive themselves to be directly affected by a decision or activity, individuals inside the organization, partners in the decision, regulators and other government organizations that have authority over activities, politicians, non-government organizations, the media and other interested individuals and groups. The stakeholder consultation process should be continuous and included as an integral part of risk communication."

Is this over-reach? I don't think so. We acknowledge that an organization's public reputation is its most important asset in our modern media-inundated world. This means communicating intelligently with these groups is the key to building and maintaining public confidence. The still-unwinding fiasco of Firestone-Bridgestone tires used on Ford vehicles is a case of an early failure of reasonable communication with customers and public regulators. The continuing news stories and recriminations damage the reputation of two global corporations. Risk communication suggests that we involve consumer and groups and regulators far earlier in the process of making operational decisions involving risk.

Three other supporting documents come from the Conference Board of Canada. "A Time to Speak—Strategic Leadership for Effective Corporate Communications" re-emphasizes the "six Rs of corporate communications—having the *right source,* and providing the *right information* to the *right audience* at the *right time* in the *right place* using the *right dissemination method.*" Karen Thiessen's "Don't Gamble with Goodwill: The Value of Effectively Communicating Risks" and "Ambassadors of Goodwill: Key Insights of Some Well-Known Case

Studies in Risk and Crisis Communication" cite three Canadian organizations that have successfully integrated risk communications in their risk management programs.

Together, these papers provide a succinct summary of developing principles and practices in risk communication. Yes, an active process with all stakeholders opens a can of worms, but those very worms should be considered the bait with which we attract and keep public confidence.

For more information on the NERAM paper, contact John Shortreed at shortree@uwaterloo.ca. For the CBC papers, contact Karen Thiessen at thiessen@conferenceboard.ca.

How Do We Communicate, and With Whom?
(January 2001)

Since decisions create risks and risks provide both benefits and harms to different groups, it is understandable that we must communicate these potentials, both positive and negative, to those affected. A failure to do so threatens the confidence of both internal (employees) and external (suppliers, customers, investors, regulators, etc.) stakeholders. Confidence, translated into reputation, is easily the most important asset of any organization. The Bridgestone-Firestone-Ford fiasco of 2000 is a classic case in point. These companies failed to communicate in advance some of their critical risks and risk decisions, making their denials, protestations and counter-claims after the fact simply unbelievable. I have argued for some time that better risk communication is a key part of the risk management process. As reader Mike Murphy, of Cadmus Consulting in Canada, recently noted, "Candid assessments of downsides in advance of an event may insulate an organization from excessive adverse reaction when something actually goes awry." He continued, "If you make enough deposits in the bank of credibility, you may be able to draw some out in an emergency." True, but how do we manage the communication of potentially bad news, when today's financial officers are scared to death that even the smallest bit of black cloud will send shareholders to the exits? JPMorgan's Bill Kelly had it right when he suggested that you "make sure that your laundry is clean before you air it!" But if it's always "clean," is it candid?

Dealing with stakeholders intelligently and honestly is a difficult art. Last year I cited Warren Buffett's candid *mea culpa* in Berkshire Hathaway's annual report, but his track record gives him considerable leeway for bad news. *CFO* created a new award last year for "Managing External Stakeholders," given to Jeff Henley, CFO of Oracle Corporation. Henley noted that he spent "much more time with customers" than with securities analysts. That's a key point. If a CRO is to be successful in communicating what an organization knows—and doesn't know—about risk, customers must be at the top of the information chain.

An excellent dissertation on practical risk communication is "Principles of Communicating Risks," by Jean Mulligan, Elaine McCoy and Angela Griffiths, published by the Macleod Institute for Environmental Analysis of the University of Calgary, in March 1998 (macleod@acs.ucalgary.ca). The authors suggest that stakeholders do not "consent to risks so much as select options . . . that strike a tolerable balance between desirable and undesirable factors." These are value judgments that may change, even radically, from one day to the next. While the paper addresses primarily environmental, health, and safety issues, its conclusions apply to *all* risks. The description of the multiplicity of stakeholders, messages, information content and the nature of risk cogently summarizes some of the critical factors in effective communication. The authors conclude, "Communicating risk successfully is neither a public relations nor a crisis communications exercise. Its aim is not to avoid all conflict or to diffuse all concerns. Risk communication seeks to improve performance based on informed, mutual decisions with respect to . . . risks." Good communication must acknowledge good faith and basic comprehension capabilities on the part of all parties.

Yet this fixation with risk communication, especially as an issue for 2001, may need a reality check. I was "brought up, all standing," to use Patrick O'Brian's nautical phrase, by Roger Kasperson's recent editorial in the *RISK Newsletter* (Fourth Quarter 2000), of the Society for Risk Analysis. Kasperson, a professor at Clark University and a past President of the Society, warned that we may have elevated risk communication to "the holy grail of risk management." He went on, "We are on the stakeholder-involvement express, barreling down the rails of well-intentioned but often naïve efforts to address growing public concerns over risks, changed public expectations over the functioning of democratic institutions, and historic declines in social trust in those responsible for protecting public safety." He sees the word "stakeholders" itself as a misnomer, one that leaves out "those who do not yet know that their interests are at stake, whose interests are diffuse or associated broadly with citizenship, who lack the skills and resources to compete, or who have simply lost confidence in the political process." We still do not know what communication interventions are likely to be successful: ". . . Participatory effectiveness is a learned skill that requires resources, it is cumulative and long-term in nature, [and] it is cultural in that it requires participatory domains in the various spheres of one's life (family, community, social networks, work, etc.)" Kasperson calls for a brake "on the current stakeholder express"—or at least a "switch to the local" so that we can be more reflective and self-critical in our risk communication efforts. This is a wise admonition, with which I agree.

My good friend Tony Benson, the retired risk manager for Guinness (now Diageo), also warns of the possible repercussions of appearing to favor stakeholders other than shareholders. He argues that risk managers "owe a primary duty to those who employ them," the owners (shareholders) of the business. I acknowledge that is the prevailing opinion. But I disagree with the word "primary." Just as we must work with all risks together, avoiding over-focus on any one, so too must we try to balance the needs, requirements and perceptions of all stakeholders, without over-concentrating on just one. Yes, investors are important, but so too are customers, suppliers, and the public! I believe that 2001 will see increased discussion of risk communication as an important organizational exercise.

One communication method gaining favor is the internal risk management intranet. First suggested by Scott Lange when he was Microsoft's Risk Manager, intranets are now in use in several major corporations, including Schlumberger, in France, and Bradford & Bingley, in England. Clive Moffatt, writing in *StrategicRisk* in September 2000, summarized some of the practical ingredients of a successful intranet: "1) Be interactive, 2) Be easy to use, 3) Have features that allow development

executives routinely exaggerate the benefits and discount the costs, setting themselves up for failure." The authors suggest this is attributable to the latent optimism that resides in all of us. A new project proposal inevitably comes with enthusiastic sponsors who overestimate its positive attributes. Similarly, these sponsors tend to "neglect the potential abilities and actions" of competitors. They assume that rivals will fail to respond or move too late. And finally, when an organization has limited funds for new projects, those selected for investment will be the ones carrying "the most over-optimistic forecasts."

Kahneman and Lovallo believe that "optimism generates much more enthusiasm than it does realism (not to mention pessimism)." Is this a new and recent phenomenon or has it always been so? I suggest this has been a continuing characteristic of our human species. The authors then provide five steps to correct the optimistic bias they say is found today in many organizations:

1. Select a "reference class" of outside data or organizations with which to compare the proposed project, and rank your idea against them.
2. Assess the distribution of outcomes of these projects/data, taking care to consider carefully the extremes.
3. Make an intuitive prediction of your project's position in the distribution.
4. Assess the reliability of your prediction.
5. Correct your intuitive estimate.

Sounds very much like traditional risk management thinking, doesn't it? Kahneman and Lovallo conclude that most managers are "likely to underestimate the overall probability of unfavorable outcomes."

A contrary opinion comes from Benjamin Hunt, a U.K. journalist. "Business is terrified of taking risk," he writes. In *The Timid Corporation* (John Wiley & Sons Ltd. 2003), Hunt argues that today's corporations are enveloped in a cloud of "irrational pessimism," and that "risk aversion has become more of a permanent mindset and mode of operation, independent of the business cycle." He sees risk aversion "institutionalized in business." Part of the blame lies with risk management itself: "The problem with the enormous rise of risk management is that it entrenches a new intolerance of risk and uncertainty." On the surface, Hunt is at odds with Kahneman and Lovallo.

The Timid Corporation is meticulously researched, including a seven-page bibliography of books and articles. Unfortunately, most of them come from the insurance and finance arenas. Hunt did not tap any of the vast resource of public policy risk management documentation. It might not have changed his gloomy prognosis, but it would have enriched it.

Hunt begins his first section by castigating the "re-regulation of the corporation," a process that entrenches caution through both external and self-regulation. He tackles briefly the problems of the risk management discipline and then suggests that managing for shareholder value creates a new form of financial risk aversion. His second section suggests that industry has adopted a "defensive mode" and that it is obsessed with the customer. Through an emphasis on brands and customer loyalty, it has "dumbed down innovation." All this leads to a "fear of growth." Finally, Hunt describes the current "crisis of self-belief" and sets forth suggestions for breaking the current paralysis.

I can't accept his entire thesis, but pieces ring true. For example, Hunt writes: "Rather than take a lead in upholding strong principles and shaping change, corporations attempt to 'listen to society' and 'listen to the customer.' But the world around them—including the business world and broader society—has also become more risk-averse at the same time, and newly demands caution and restraint in behaviour." This is a valid point—corporations are a part of the culture and it is undeniably more cautious today than a decade ago. After the shocks of the breaking stock market bubble and the advent of global terrorism, a fresh emphasis on regulation is understandable. But Hunt says that the "holy trinity of accountability, responsibility and transparency" has moved too far. The precautionary principle in public affairs has been adopted by business: do not experiment unless the outcome is safe and poses no risks. Hunt equally criticizes self-regulation and the rise of interest in ethics and corporate governance. I agree with him when he writes: "Just repeating the term corporate governance more than a few times in one day can make lips seize up with dryness!"

Then Hunt argues that listening to society can be irrational, citing the example of the Brent Spar fiasco. True, but that case and others similar to it do not mean that it is improper to engage other stakeholders in serious discussions about risk. I believe that it is worthwhile, over time, to reach out to the public and especially to non-government organizations (NGOs), even when they spread nonsense.

The author's dissection of risk management, also, is both savage and incomplete. Yes, too many insurance and financial risk managers are paranoid about uncertainty and act as the resident corporate nay-sayers. And managers can be easily frustrated when "highly tedious, door-stopper-like risk management manuals land with a thump on their desk(s), and they are asked to wade through them before making a decision." But most of today's risk management practitioners can entwine logical and reasonable risk analyses within their organizations without recourse to monumental tomes. Hunt's history of risk management is flawed as it is almost entirely related to its development within insurance. His notes indicate that he interviewed 14 "risk managers," but, from the tone of this chapter, most of them must have been insurance risk managers, leaving out credit, market, public policy and other operational risk practitioners. He cites no names or titles, so I cannot be sure. Hunt also perpetuates the discarded and thoroughly discredited distinction between "passive" and "speculative" risks, a construction of the insurance industry to avoid taking on risk with which it was unfamiliar. Most observers today accept that risk involves both upside and downside potentials and that trying to separate them into distinct packages is a disservice to the idea of treating risk holistically.

Hunt's attack on the "new obsession with the customer" goes too far. When Ralph Nader wrote *Unsafe at Any Speed* in the 1960s, the prevailing legal dictum was *caveat emptor*—let the buyer beware. Nader argued successfully that much more was required of the selling corporation, and the consumer movement began. Today, largely as a result of Nader's continuing work, the current dictum is *caveat vendor*—let the seller beware. Perhaps the pendulum has swung too far, especially with litigation in the United States, but it has redressed a prior imbalance. Hunt's argument that today's corporation is fixated on customer loyalty and brand protection may be true, but I'm not ready to accept the conclusion of his syllogism that this leads to the stagnation of innovation and a fear of growth. I do agree with his identification of a major current irony: "Just at a time when managers and corporations see the world as more risky and unpredictable and are more defensive, a range of commentators view corporations as wanting aggressively to 'take over' the world."

Hunt argues that a social climate of risk aversion affects corporations, but does this instill excessive caution in *all* of them? I admit to being more of an optimist: it's only a temporary mode. I do agree with his two suggestions for change: take a more critical attitude toward regulation and self-regulation, and raise expectations of technological progress. The latter *will* occur and will shift us out of our malaise! Finally, Hunt is right when he writes that "in this world, it is worth bearing in mind that a society that does not try to shape its future ends up being dictated to by its anxieties."

So we have two views of our current situation. One says that organizations are too risk avaricious, the other that we are too risk averse. Take your pick!

> *The ideal is to draw a clear distinction between those functions and positions that involve or support decision-making and those that promote or guide action. The former should be imbued with a realistic outlook, while the latter will often benefit from a sense of optimism.*
>
> **Dan Lovallo and Daniel Kahneman,**
> **"Delusions of Success,"** *Harvard Business Review,* **July 2003**

CHAPTER 9

Insurance

*A*s I first approached risk management from my personal education and experience in insurance, I've always had a critical view of this industry. I tend to see its flaws more readily than its strengths, for which I apologize. But, having stepped away from insurance in 1970, I remain an interested and continuing observer, as these essays show.

Oh Insurer, Where Art Thou?
(April 2002)

Is it possible to shoot yourself in the foot and then put your bloody foot in your mouth, doubling your agony? The non-life (property and casualty) insurance business may have performed that feat, in the aftermath of September 11 and the Enron collapse.

Consider these news items, all of which suggest an amazing inability of the insurance industry to sustain any sort of credibility with its policyholders and the public:

(1) Four major contracting firms cleaning up the debris of the World Trade Center bombing and collapse in New York can't buy any commercial liability insurance. They are "too risky," according to insurance companies declining to underwrite them, led by Liberty Mutual and American International Group (AIG). Didn't these insurers consider the adverse publicity that would follow this decision?

(2) CEOs of the leading U.S. insurers and reinsurers rushed to Washington after September 11, pleading for government financing for terrorism

coverage, arguing that, should another attack occur, the industry could collapse. Congress stalled. Economists cautioned that government should stay away from terrorist coverage. By March 2002 one leading insurance executive changed tacks and tried to persuade the government to back out of the limited protection that it had offered U.S. airlines. Do they need help or don't they?

(3) A major reinsurer sues the owner of the Twin Towers, arguing that the event is a single loss, not two. Its argument may be right, but bringing a highly visible lawsuit is lousy public relations.

(4) Eleven insurance companies refuse to pay for surety bonds issued to JPMorganChase as performance guarantees for Enron oil-and-gas derivatives contracts, suggesting that these were disguised as outright loans. A judge agrees with this contention and the case goes to trial. The bank has no interim surety payment. The refusals generate more newspaper headlines.

(5) Two insurers try to void directors' and officers' liability policies they wrote for Enron, alleging "misrepresentation." The explanations of "misrepresentation" are "vague," according to *The New York Times,* creating the perception that this is another attempt by insurers to avoid claim payments.

(6) Directors are threatened not only with non-payment by their Directors' & Officers' policy insurers but also by the suggestion of Treasury Secretary, Paul O'Neill, that the government should completely disallow the use of insurance to cover lawsuits alleging director and officer misconduct. Could the entire D & O market be scuttled?

(7) Insurance companies levy massive rate increases, offer reduced limits, and add new policy exclusions, arguing that crippling losses threaten their existence. At the same time, investors are throwing upwards of US$27 billion in new money into the business, lured by promised huge profits in the next few years. Who is right? How are policyholders likely to respond?

(8) Conning & Co. publishes a new research report suggesting that U.S. insurance company reserves are deficient by US$16 billion. This has been an almost chronic criticism over the past ten years. Is the industry really this far off in its reserving practices?

(9) AIG, one of the companies leading the U.S. Congressional charge for

financial relief, is now the subject of critical evaluation. *The Economist* (March 2, 2002): writes that "... conflicts of interest on Wall Street, impenetrable accounting, the offshore registration of corporate vehicles, large financial exposures, unhealthy deference given to celebrity chief executives and high share valuations [are all] concerns germane to AIG ... AIG has yet publicly to anoint a successor, clear up its overseas registrations, find a way to provide confidence in accounting for derivatives, and persuade investors that it is properly scrutinized by regulators." It goes on to say the AIG market valuation is US$100 billion too high. The next week Sanford Bernstein argues that the valuation is US$50 billion too low! Who is right?

(10) Lack of underwriting skill, say many observers, is the primary ingredient in the huge insurance underwriting losses of the past decade. Now new money is being shoveled into the same hands. Will it slip through just as fast? Where will the industry find qualified underwriters? An ad seeking an "active underwriter" for a "start-up Lloyd's composite syndicate" appears in *The Economist* on February 9, 2002. This creates little sense of confidence that the industry knows what it is doing.

(11) Insurance broker Marsh creates a new insurer named Axis Specialty, displaying a total lack of historical memory. Don't brokers read the history of World War II? Then President Bush uses the phrase "axis of evil" in his January 2002 State of the Union address. When will Marsh change the Axis name? Why not try "Enron" or "Andersen?" Both may be available shortly.

(12) Marsh also initially offered the families of the employees lost on September 11 one year of continued health insurance. Publicity and complaints followed. It then offered the coverage for three years, deducting the additional costs from the fund it had established for these families. More uproar. Now it promises to pay all these costs directly. Didn't anyone think before acting?

(13) In London last fall, the House of Lords settled an appeal on a case involving Aneco, a Bermuda-based reinsurer, and Johnson & Higgins (now part of Marsh). The brokerage firm tried to serve as broker for both a Lloyd's syndicate and Aneco on the same transaction, a blatant

conflict of interest. The wearing of two hats is ludicrous but it is still common practice.

(14) The insurance brokerage community continues to be unwilling to eliminate other conflicts of interest that burden its relationships. It steadfastly tries to maintain the status quo of serving a client and being paid by the vendor that it chooses for that client. It adds to this mess by accepting profit, bonus and other commissions and holding insurer funds for its own interest income. Brokers also blur relationships by creating their own insurers (see Axis above). Now the Enron scandal highlights the insidious use of "facilitation payments," a euphemism for bribes. As *The Economist* wrote in early March 2002, "Accepting small gifts, invitations to lavish events or the loan of someone's luxury car can soon lead to bigger things, in a vicious circle of *quid pro quo* . . . Today's facilitation payment is tomorrow's bribe." These so-called "small" gifts are endemic to the insurance world. When will buyers and sellers wake up to their pernicious effects?

Am I over-reacting? I admit that the insurance industry fed and schooled me for thirteen years, before I shifted to risk management consulting and writing over 32 years ago. I hesitate to bite this once-generous hand. But the yawning abyss between how the industry sees itself and how others see it is too glaring. For example, Patrick Liedtke and Christophe Courbage, writing in the Geneva Association's *Information Newsletter* for January 2002 suggest that September 11 "could turn not only into the most costly in insurance history; it might also become the finest hour for the industry." What publications and materials have they been reading? Another writer, in the February *CFO*, comments "few blame the insurance industry for rushing to the exits." Really? The general press (not the insurance press) is full of irate customers chastising the industry and seeking more rational and economic alternatives. Orio Giarini writes in the December 2001 *Progres,* also from the Geneva Association, "Once again we see how far the insurance industry has moved toward the center of the economic and social picture." I suggest that the movement is entirely opposite!

Why is it that this industry—potentially so valuable to so many throughout the world, and with such a rich history—has a death wish, a desire to alienate its customers and marginalize itself? Why is it that when a loss occurs, especially a large one, the insurance industry tends to present the face of a reluctant dragon? I acknowledge that this is not a universal reaction—in the Hurricane Andrew and Oakland fire aftermaths, insurance companies responded quickly and generously to those sustaining losses. Yet in the corporate world, it carries a reputation of slow and questioning payments, coupled with volatility in both pricing and coverage that perplexes buyers seeking greater stability.

It's a problem. Insurers, where are you when we need you?

Kudos to Insurance
(December 2002)

I've criticized the insurance industry for many of its business practices, yet all is not gloom and doom. In keeping with this holiday season I wish to report two examples of *good* management. The business *can* be run well.

On the dark and stormy evening of Tuesday, October 15, 2002, a woman with whom I am closely acquainted (but who shall remain anonymous) backed her station wagon into a remarkably sturdy mailbox, shattering her rear window but leaving the box mutely testifying its superiority. The next morning I reported the accident by phone to her insurer, the United Services Automobile Association (USAA), in San Antonio, Texas, and took the car to the local dealer for repair. We returned from a short trip two days later (late Friday) and collected the repaired car. On Monday morning I reported the claim costs to the USAA telephone representative, who noted them and the applicable deductible, and advised that a check would be sent immediately. On Friday, October 25, the USAA check arrived, four days after reporting the cost of the claim and nine after the initial report. I spent all of seven minutes on the telephone.

While I treat this as exceptional service, I'm sure that USAA views it as standard, as it should.

My second example: the risk manager of a major financial institution in New York City reported to me the following: "To give you an example of how topsy-turvy the insurance markets are these days, we just completed a casualty (insurance) renewal in which every party to the transaction—the broker, the winning insurer, my company, and even the losing incumbent broker—ended up very happy with the outcome. If I recall, Jerry Seinfeld joked about a hidden world within our world where everything is reversed. It appears that we have all taken a temporary trip into this universe."

My first example shows how an organization can turn a normal service relationship into one that is noteworthy. The second shows how times of stress and misgivings can be turned to mutual benefit. Trust and confidence in service are the goals of good risk management.

> . . . having uncertainty [is] the value of having the openness of possibility.
>
> **Richard P. Feynman, *The Meaning of It All,***
> **Helix Books, Reading, Massachusetts 1998**

A "Nightmare Scenario"?
(August 2003)

Early in July, I read a delicious phrase in *The Economist*. It called luxury goods "ludicrously expensive inessentials." As I was then preparing my annual review of the insurance industry, it occurred to me that this phrase could apply to a reeling global giant. Is it possible that its skyrocketing premiums and growing financial insecurity will make its products and services no longer essential or even useful?

For the past few years I've devoted at least one piece a year to my observations of the insurance world. In 2001 it was "The Unraveling" (*RMR* December 2001), describing the industry's tailspin following the events of September 11. In 2002, I continued with "Insurer, Where Art Thou?" (*RMR* April 2002), outlining a mounting skepticism about the ability of property-casualty insurers to regain both profitability and buyer confidence.

This year's view is even less sanguine. My title is taken from a short report from Aon and Oxford Metrica, prepared by Dr. Deborah Pretty, in which she suggests that the combination of the aftermath of September

11, the stock market plunge and the need to increase reserves has created a "nightmare scenario of unprecedented proportions for the industry." I agree. Continuing adverse losses, inadequate underwriting, reserve deficiencies, problems with reinsurance recoveries, an uncertain stock and bond market, an inability to contain operating expenses and horrible press coverage combine to offset almost entirely the radical, if not irresponsible, rate increases dumped on buyers in the past two years. First, during the 90s, the lemmings rushed to undercut prices and offer the moon. Now these same lemmings swing to the opposite extreme, perhaps leaping over the cliff to their mutual destruction! The news isn't reassuring:

- Despite monumental price increases, the statutory operating expense ratio of U.S. property-casualty insurers, according to A.M. Best report for 2002, remains at an astronomical 38%, dropping but three points from 41% in 2001. How can an industry survive with this overhead cost, one that leaves only 62% of premiums to pay for losses? This is incredible inefficiency.
- According to A.M. Best, the combined ratio (losses and expenses compared to premiums) for U.S. insurers was just under 100% for the first quarter of 2003, the first time since 1986 the industry has produced a profit on underwriting. Yet its statutory return on investment is only 8.8% as compared to the general stock market goal of 15%. With these meager returns and the overhanging threat of massive replenishment of reserves, can the industry attract new capital?
- Some observers predict that underwriters will relax their prices in light of this newfound marginal profitability. Lower rates could mean more underwriting losses, moving the lemmings ever closer to the precipice.
- "The insurance industry is in poor shape, particularly in Europe," reports The Economist (March 8, 2003). An insurer is more likely than a bank to go under in today's economy, particularly in Germany, Britain and Switzerland. The reasons: mispriced underwriting, poor investment performance and "messy regulation," among others. That newspaper's conclusion: "Insurers today look like the weakest link in the finance-industry chain."

- Dr. Pretty, in another Oxford Metrica report released on June 30, 2003, cites a continuing exposure to long-tailed liabilities causing the downward trend in financial strength ratings. Clearly this year's early favorable numbers do not fool the analysts. As she points out, "The creditworthiness of risk bearers" requires the immediate attention of corporate buyers of insurance.
- Earlier this year Conning & Co. warned that the "reserve deficiency" of the U.S. market increased from US$16 billion in 2001 to $38.5 billion at the end of 2002. Some companies responded: Hartford tripled its asbestos reserves to a total of $5.97 billion; Travelers added $1.3 billion; AIG added $1.8 billion; ACE $2.2 billion and other companies followed suit. But is it enough?
- Willis, in its *Global Perspectives 2003,* called the property/casualty market an "anemic patient."

Consider some of the specific problems that face both buyers and sellers of insurance.

- *Asbestos*: The continuing threat of asbestosis equally affects insurers, reinsurers and insureds. Many corporations have declared bankruptcy to protect themselves from the avalanche of claims. A RAND Corporation study illustrates the magnitude of this litigation. From 1982 to 2001, claimants ballooned from 21,000 to more than 600,000. Total costs to date are US$54 billion, but are estimated to soar as high as $145 to $210 billion. Washington finally reacted with a Congressional proposal to establish a national combined trust fund to pay all current and future claimants—a fund that will be financed by corporate and insurance contributions. Trust fund or not, the costs will be horrendous and the effect on the insurance industry enormous. Add to this that we are rapidly exporting to other countries an over-aggressive plaintiffs' bar.
- *Wall Street*: In the aftermath of the stock-market plunge, investors cry foul, blaming blatant deception by rapacious brokers and analysts. Several major investment firms have settled the initial regulatory lawsuits to the tune of $1.4 billion, some of which will

be passed to insurers as claims. In addition these same firms must now settle with their customers, suggesting a spiraling of losses far in excess of the initial payments to regulators. Add these potential D&O losses to insurer reserves!

- *Floods*: The disastrous floods of 2002 in Europe totaled more than 17 billion euros, but, of this amount, only 2.8 billion Euros were insured. Insurance thus played a minor role (16%) in these catastrophes. Yet even these insured losses savaged insurer and reinsurer results. Could the insurance industry have handled a 17 billion Euro loss? Probably not. Buyers will now think twice about using conventional insurance as a financing mechanism for catastrophe losses. Governments, including the EU, have stepped in to create funds to deal with similar future disasters. Will conventional insurers expand their underwriting and sales to cover such losses in the future? Probably not. And so the industry becomes even more marginalized.

- *Mismanagement*: The collapse of HIH in Australia produced a governmental inquiry that has placed 90 directors, managers, auditors and actuaries under scrutiny, according to *Asia Insurance Review*. This sort of indictment raises serious questions about *all* management in the industry.

- *Sexual Abuse*: The outpouring of sexual abuse claims against the Roman Catholic Church in the United States (and to a lesser extent in Europe) means more requests to insurers for reimbursement. Worse than that, several Archdioceses have used every means at their disposal to try and deny or reduce claims, even as they argue that they prefer to settle out of court. Why? Their lawyers argue that their insurance policy terms require them to use all possible defense mechanisms before a claim will be accepted. If this allegation is true, buyers will see insurance playing a counter-productive role. To collect any insurance, a claimant must work against its own best interests, and those of the injured parties, just to satisfy a contractual policy requirement. The attempt to protect future insurance recoveries further destroys the insured's reputation and the public's confidence. What value, then, is insurance?

- *Credit*: Another ominous cloud is the potential for insurers and reinsurers to be tagged with bank credit losses. Over the past few years, many insurers and reinsurers bought credit derivatives from banks, ostensibly to improve their investments returns. According to *The Economist*, these derivatives reached US$60 billion by the end of 2002—equivalent to 8% of all commercial and industrial credit portfolios. If the global economy continues to sag, imagine the fresh claims against insurer capital! As *The Economist* commented "the possible fragility of credit-derivatives markets (has) yet to be fully tested." It concluded: "Savour this moment while it lasts."

- *Service*: It was inexcusable to me in 1971, when I first wrote about it, and it continues to be inexcusable. Why can't insurance companies deliver a policy of insurance, complete and accurate, along with a premium invoice, in advance of the inception date? It happened to me again this spring. While USAA continues to deliver both policy and bill for my personal insurance *before* inception, most other insurers are chronically unable to complete this simple task. I ordered from another company a liability policy for a nonprofit I serve on May 28, 2003. I received a binder and invoice on June 17, but, as of July 30, I have no policy in hand! Even worse, I ordered a marine policy from a third agent in January for a June renewal and received a quote. On the renewal date I called the agent to ask about the cover. He explained that the quote was no longer valid (it lasted only three months!) and that now I needed a full survey *before* another quote and coverage would be provided. Am I an exception to good service? I think not, based on similar horror stories I hear all the time

Governments, nonprofits and corporations don't sit by idly, watching this drama unfold. They take action, much of which removes significant risk funds from traditional insurance. Increased deductibles and self-insurance are common. Consider terrorism insurance, for example. After 9/11, insurers and reinsurers introduced terrorism exclusions. When the U.S. Congress passed legislation (the U.S. Terrorist Risk Insurance Act of 2002) that provided a measure of indemnification for future terrorist losses, underwriters reinstated some coverage—but on an optional basis with an additional premium. Guess what? Buyers aren't buying! The Hartford reported that 85% of its insureds turned down the coverage and additional premium, and others report a similar disinclination. Most insureds don't believe that they face a serious exposure, as they think it is confined to major cities and infrastructure locations. It is a classic case of adverse selection—something that the underwriters should have foreseen.

Consider the French as another example. Their insurance risk managers have proposed a new industry-owned stock insurer capitalized at 50 million Euros to underwrite property and business interruption exposures in the 15-25 million Euro range. While this new company hardly solves major capacity and cost problems—it's too small to do anything but become a minor partner with the ogre they wish to displace— the idea is sound. It could (and should) be beefed up to a capitalization of at least 1 billion Euros should the basic numbers make sense. The Bermuda-based insurers XL and ACE began in a similar fashion in the last high-priced insurance market and it follows a tradition of do-it-yourself that started in the United States in the mid-1800s when a group of ship-owners, unhappy with the marine insurance rates of Lloyds, created Atlantic Mutual.

Another response example is the use of captive insurers. High prices, limited capacity, and restrictive terms and conditions whet the appetite to create a captive. Interest and applications are up, according to managers and domicile regulators, but most current and potential owners face the same problems as the insurance managers in France. Their captives are too small to undertake significant loss exposures. They are corporate toys. Couple that with the lack of both fronting insurance (an insurer legally licensed in a needed jurisdiction) and affordable reinsurance— and add the fresh attention of legislatures to squash tax loopholes—and the captive situation is not encouraging. *Captive Insurance Company Reports* (May 2003) noted that a "mutual suspicion . . . now exists between providers and captive owners. The fronting provider suspects the security of the captive and its parent; the captive owner suspects the security of the fronting company!" Although single-parent captives may do little to defuse the cost-coverage situation, group-owned insurers could provide some relief and set the stage for a mass exodus of funding from the traditional market.

And finally, there is the example set by Warren Buffett. According to *The Economist*, when faced with seemingly irrational rate escalations in Directors' and Officers' Liability insurance, he decided not to buy protection for the board of Berkshire Hathaway, a company that includes several insurers in its stable. His idea? Scrap the by-laws that indemnify directors and let them buy their own coverage. That may reduce the pool of available directors, but it will produce more responsible ones! This could be the beginning of a change in buying habits that materially affects the market.

Now consider the bad press received by the insurance industry. I think much is self-inflicted. A knee-jerk reaction of cancellations, exclusions and price increases in the United States followed 9/11, much of it without communication with policyholders. Asian insurers gave us a similar knee-jerk reaction of after SARS hit. According to *Asia Insurance Review* (June 2003), many said they would not cover SARS-related claims. Some Australian travel insurance companies specifically deleted coverage. Then the more aggressive firms turned around and offered special policies—those that provide US$50,000 for *both* SARS *and* terrorist attacks! Exclude the exposure and then offer a special, new, high-priced policy to cover it! That does not enhance the reputation of an industry that purports to be there when you need it. Did anyone consider how potential buyers react to these stories? The same issue reported the CEO of a major Japanese insurer stating, "Insurers can meet the needs of society by providing medical and healthcare insurance, contributing to the prevention of accidents, maintaining a high standard of morals for good corporate governance, and even providing covers against catastrophic risks such as flood and terrorism." When buyers contrast platitudes such as this with the continuing headlines of mismanagement, cancellations, exclusions, and financial insecurity, they begin to wonder.

It was no different in Ireland, where a spate of recent cancellations and price increases reached news reporters, making insurance a "hot topic," according to a *New York Times* analysis. It resulted in a national effort to create a Personal Injuries Assessment Board to weigh injury claims and award formula-based compensation. This proposed board effectively removes claims management from insurers. The Irish don't trust insurers to settle their own claims.

Medical doctors in three U.S. states symbolically "walked out" this year in protest against increasing medical malpractice insurance premiums, provoking front page headlines all over the United States and a move in Congress to limit awards. Regardless of the merits of the case involving physicians, claimants and plaintiffs lawyers, the news reports have uniformly cast a negative cloud over insurance companies. They are accused of investment mismanagement, draconian premium increases, and sloppy defense, allegations, whether true or not, repeated in many news stories. One major underwriter, the St. Paul Companies, exited the market and others plan to do the same. It is the same story—the insurance industry sits by while cast in the role of perpetual villain.

Not only the national press is dangerous—local editorials do even more damage. "Insurance companies, it seems, are increasingly risk-averse these days," said the editor of *Working Waterfront* (June 2003), a paper in Maine. The accompanying article reported that many owners of properties on islands could no longer get *any* insurance, even at escalated premiums, allegedly because of their remote locations. Even though most islands have volunteer fire departments as efficient as those on the mainland—a frame dwelling is likely to burn to the ground in either location—it seems to islanders (and to others) that insurance underwriters are seeking any excuse not to write insurance. This is the message that comes across in these local papers.

So what is the state of the insurance union this summer of 2003? It is infirm but the disease is not terminal. Have I selected some of the more egregious negative examples? I plead guilty. I admit that I've taken those examples that illustrate a central theme of an industry, especially in the United States, that is mistrusted for its underwriting, its claims-payment practices, its operational efficiency and its financial security, by experts and the laity alike. Is this, however, a "nightmare scenario" in which traditional insurance becomes "inessential," to be replaced by other means of risk financing? I am not as pessimistic as I may sound. I believe that the global property and casualty insurance business has sufficient inherent strength to overcome these current difficulties. The reason that I've been a continuing critic of its deficiencies is that I maintain an underlying belief that it can, and will, resurrect itself, with fresh leadership. Insurance remains an important part of the global financial community but it must recognize that it is only one of a number of possible solutions to loss financing. It requires radical surgery to change its basic operating procedures. It requires consolidation. It requires more intelligent regulation, global, national and local. And it requires a fresh approach to service to its customers. Only then can it reestablish public confidence in its products and services.

A nightmare is but a dream from which we awake, thankful that it is not reality.

> *At the most we gaze at it in wonder, a kind of wonder which in itself is a form of dawning horror, for somehow we know by instinct that outsize buildings cast the shadow of their own destruction before them, and are designed from the first with an eye to their later existence as ruins.*
> W. G. Sebald, *Austerlitz*, Modern Library, New York 2001

Fatalism and Conflicts of Interest
(June 2004)

I'm becoming a fatalist in my old age. Late in April several readers asked for my thoughts on the recent disclosure that the Attorneys General in New York and Connecticut and the Insurance Commissioner in California are investigating alleged conflicts of interest surrounding contingency commissions received by several major insurance brokerage firms. I suppose I should have replied, like the good Inspector in *Casablanca,* "I'm shocked, shocked!" These revelations, however, are old and stale—several of us have railed against the patent misrepresentations and egregious interest conflicts inherent in the global "system" of insurance sales for more than thirty years, to little effect. My cynical comment is that matters won't change this time around.

The problem lies in how an insurance broker presents its services to the public. It claims, for example, that it is the "representative" of its client, offering experience, judgment and expertise in selecting and placing the most appropriate insurance for that client. Yet who pays the broker? The insurance company awards the broker a commission, one that is negotiated almost entirely by the broker and the company. Does this distort the placement process, when one company offers a commission higher than another, or when one (a mutual) offers no commission? No, say the brokers—we are entirely and completely objective! Then consider what the Attorneys General are studying: most brokers also arrange additional commissions—euphemistically known as "placement service agreements"—should a piece of business be especially coveted by a company or if an entire book of business placed by that broker delivers a profit in excess of agreed margins. Do these "contingency commissions" affect placement decisions? "Of course not," protest the brokers. They are merely an "age-old and common practice" (from an Aon spokesman— *New York Times*), "a long-standing, common industry practice" (the CEO of Marsh—also *New York Times*) or a "reward system when the job is done right" (a letter to *Business Insurance* by the CEO of a New York brokerage firm). If we've been doing it for years, how can it be unethical or even illegal?

But the list of under-the-table payments hardly ends with the upfront and contingency commissions. Brokers conventionally collect the premiums due insurers and may hold these fiduciary funds for several days or as long as several months, earning interest for the broker's account— not for the insured or insurer. If they hold a strong negotiating position, they can demand the right to place any facultative reinsurance for a particular client's insurance program, thus generating more commissions. Some brokers receive low-interest loans from insurers. One insurer took a major stock position in a publicly held broker. And brokers have invested in the creation of new insurers with which they then place business.

The problem today isn't that most buyers don't know what is going on. They know but they don't care. "Our members appreciate what the broker is doing. They don't care where the payments are coming from as long as they are disclosed," protested the executive director of the Risk & Insurance Management Society (RIMS), the representative organization of insurance buyers, as quoted in the *New York Times*. Are these buyers therefore complicit in supporting this system of conflicts by not raising the hue and cry for change? Yes—even though RIMS some five years ago gently slapped the brokers' wrists and asked them, please, to disclose these arrangements when asked!

Admittedly, the "system" that countenances these manifest conflicts has been working well for more than 150 years, so why change it? Most insurance brokers that I know display a remarkable level of objectivity, given these multiple payments generated from their vendors, not their clients. Is there really any need for change now? Yes, because these payments add to the cost of insurance. Some, perhaps, go to valuable work on behalf of either the insurance company or the insured, but financial analysts allege that most of these extra payments drop directly to the brokers' bottom lines. Another roadblock is the size and clout of the few major brokerage firms—a buyer trying to attack this system may find his organization without access to needed insurance. My hope is that, just possibly, the change in current attitudes toward conflicts of interest may stimulate some systemic change.

In 1971, in *Best's Review,* I wrote the following words: "Many of the national brokerage houses operate as both brokers and agents, depending on the circumstances. Under certain agreements, they have negotiated additional contingency commission arrangements in which they will share with the insurance company the 'profit,' if any, accruing from a favorable overall loss ratio. If a broker is representing himself as serving his client, there is no moral or economic reason for him to collect a contingency commission from an insurance company. The risk manager can insist that his broker eliminate all contingency commission arrangements with the insurance companies with which he places business." I also suggested, back in 1971, that insureds should pay their brokers fees for the work they do and remit premiums directly to insurers. Thirteen years later, in 1984, I tried once more to stimulate change. I published a picture of the grin of the Cheshire Cat, with each tooth representing a broker's source of income, most from insurers. In 1998, I again rose to the bait. In "Yogi Berra, All Over Again?" (*RMR* August 1998), I argued that simple disclosure and transparency could and would not change a system corrupted by conflicts. The critical issue is that conventional insurance carries an overhead cost of from 20% to as high as 40% of premiums, the bulk of which are payments to those who "produce" and sell the insurance! That alone should indicate to buyers that the system is not working! When less than 60% of premiums are allocated to the payment of losses, it is no wonder that financial officers look at other risk financing options.

Times have changed. Now stockbrokers are guilty of unethical behavior in touting the stocks of companies that reward their firms with other fees and commissions. Mutual funds are guilty of unethical behavior for permitting favored investors to practice market timing. So why aren't insurance brokers equally guilty of unethical behavior for accepting extra payments from insurance companies, disclosed or not? Will the phrase "independent broker" join "independent agent" as an oxymoron as hilarious as "airline food?" These additional payments create the perception that the buyer's interests are not paramount to a broker.

These system participants—buyers, brokers and insurers alike—have too long tolerated a system that creaks with conflicts, anachronisms, and inefficiencies. I don't see anything "illegal" in these machinations, other than, perhaps, false advertising. But isn't it time we cleaned up the act? Today, financial services industries are forced to become more open and transparent. Even a *perception* of conflict of interest is not tolerated. So perhaps Eliot Spitzer of New York, Richard Blumenthal of Connecticut and John Garamendi of California will be the catalysts for a long-overdue change, one that has clients paying brokers directly and solely, buyers remitting premiums directly to insurers, and expenses dropping as a result. Is this too much to hope for? Probably. My fatalism caught the persistent grin of that Cheshire Cat. I hope I won't be echoing these same comments ten years from now.

> *If a risk manager desires a relationship of utmost good faith with an advisory organization, then the compensation paid by the client should be only in the form of a mutually agreeable fee. No other forms of remuneration, including contingency and reinsurance commissions, are acceptable.*
> **Felix Kloman, "Yogi Berra, All Over Again?"**
> *Risk Management Reports,* **August 1998**

Contingency Commissions and Conflicts of Interest
(November 2004)

In June 2004, *The Economist* wrote a story on the Abu Ghraib prisoner abuse, expressing disbelief at what had happened, at the internal legal memo on which the US administration based its defense, and at a weirdly perverted view of international law on torture. It saw two vicious and debilitating presumptions—first that a CEO could be above the law when faced with an extreme situation, and second that the "law" may be stretched to accommodate your prevailing current position. This piece, entitled appropriately "What on earth were they thinking?" applies to some current news coming from the United States. First, no one is above the law, even *in extremis*. Second, the idea is to obey the *spirit* of the law, not seek loopholes and excuses, such as "others do it" or "we've always done it that way."

I recalled that perceptive article as I read, with mounting dismay, the story of the mid-October lawsuit brought by the Attorney General of New York State, Eliot Spitzer, against Marsh, the world's largest insurance brokerage firm. He accuses the broker of "cheating customers by rigging prices" and accepting "kickbacks" in the form of commissions from insurers contingent on the volume, timing and profitability of certain insurance business.

That the prevalence and size of contingency commissions ultimately led to the type of alleged bid rigging can hardly be a surprise to anyone. For years, I've watched and criticized this charade of insurance brokers professing to "serve their clients" while enriching their own purses with all manner of behind-the-scenes payoffs. At first they argued that these payoffs were part of a private contract between broker and insurer, none of the business of the buyer. Then they pompously pronounced that they would *disclose* the fact that these commissions existed, although they would not allocate income specifically to any single account. When the name "contingency commissions" began to exude an offensive odor, they resorted to euphemisms, changing their name to "placement service agreements." When that title started to smell, they called them "market service agreements." These name changes alone suggest that their leaders were well aware of the real and potential conflicts.

As my readers know, I have been sharply critical of these arrangements for more than 35 years, frequently in the pages of *Risk Management Reports* (see August 1995, January 1996, August 1998, June 2004 and September 2004). I even attacked them in the late 1960s when I was still employed by an insurance brokerage firm. Contingency commissions of any type, and even the commission system itself, where the seller—not the buyer—remunerates the intermediary, and where the intermediary professes to represent *solely* the buyer, corrupt a relationship that must be built on complete trust. I have no complaint whatsoever with the payment of commissions of all types to those who present themselves as *agents* of the seller. It is the blatant misrepresentation that has fueled the Attorney General's lawsuit, plus the purported evidence of outright bid rigging.

As complete as the lawsuit's allegations are, they fail to include two other traditional mechanisms for lining the pockets of brokers—both of which, I understand are now being investigated. The first is the investment of premiums—fiduciary funds belonging to insurers—by the brokers for their own account before they are remitted to the insurance companies. This practice, however, is slowly being throttled by the insistence of insurers on direct payment of premiums. The second is the broker's ability to require that facultative reinsurance on some large placements be funneled through their own reinsurance brokerages, creating additional commissions, unreported to the original clients.

The lawsuit does note the enormous competitive advantage of the three largest insurance brokerage firms in the placement of commercial insurance business. That size and clout appear to have led directly to the alleged infractions. Is it time to break them up?

What is more disturbing is that it has taken this long for the situation to be brought to a head. Why? Because, in simple terms, the three parties to these insurance transactions have been in cahoots. Remember the admonition of Deep Throat in the newspaper investigation of the Watergate break in? He advised the reporters to "follow the money." Eliot Spitzer is doing the same. The easy dollars to trace are the additional payments from insurers to brokers—to grease the way for desired business. The more difficult dollars are those from the brokers to the buyers, making them as complicit in this sordid business as the other two. Corporate insurance buyers have willingly accepted broker contributions in the form of sponsored lunches, sponsored conferences, golf outings, sports events, and similar gratuities to their local chapters. Their national organization—the euphemistically titled Risk and Insurance Management Society (RIMS)—generates more than half of its annual operating budget not from member dues but from its annual conference, where insurance brokers contribute the lion's share through lavish exhibition booths, hospitality suites, gala dinners, tours, tournaments and direct sponsorships of breakfasts, lunches and giveaways. When so much largesse is distributed, how can these buyers possibly complain about "the system?" One of my readers asked, "Do you think risk managers are naïve, ignorant, tolerant, or what, on this issue?" The answer, unfortunately, is, "All of the above." I acknowledge that a vocal and critical minority has, for many years, tried to change this system but it has been unable to persuade the other, larger group of insurance buyers to move.

Can the system be changed? I suggested in September that a decision by a large broker and a large insurance company (AIG, for example) to terminate the practice of contingency commissions could cascade throughout the industry. Marsh first announced its "suspension" of the practice, and now says it will terminate contingency commissions altogether. ACE and American International Group (AIG) have announced that they will "likely" cease paying contingent commissions. Aon and Willis, the second and third largest brokers, will no longer accept these commissions on a global basis. But how can these firms survive a loss of income that, in some cases, is reported to be 50% of their annual net? The reduction of income to these three is over US$1 billion! Won't they, behind the scenes, try to arrange higher base commissions?

This lawsuit and the publicity attendant thereto are the catalysts we've been awaiting for thirty years. How can this system be improved? One suggestion is to substitute negotiated fees for all commissions, based on actual hours expended for a client, to be paid by buyers to brokers. Fees should be the *sole* remuneration of brokers. A second is direct negotiation between insurers and buyers, with advisors serving the buyers on the side. Scrapping the contingency commission system in its entirety is the third. As Marsh, Willis, Aon, ACE and AIG have all moved in this direction, it could become the new standard. Others will undoubtedly follow. While all these avenues are possible, they require a wrenching change in attitudes and systems. Will these changes remove the possibility of kickbacks, deals and rigging bids? No, as these failures are part of human nature. But they could reduce their frequency. The goal, however, is to begin to re-establish the relationships of trust and "utmost good faith" that are essential to purchasing insurance.

The real losers in this perverted charade are the shareholders of the corporations, the taxpayers of the governmental bodies and the donors and clients of the nonprofits that buy insurance through this archaic system. How this mess will play out over the ensuing months, I can't judge, but perhaps we may find a way to improve the system.

What on earth were they thinking?

> *What people greatly desire to believe is as interesting as truth,*
> *and generally it is more immediately influential.*
>
> **Robertson Davies, *A Merry Heart*,**
> **McClelland & Stewart, Toronto 1996**

CHAPTER 10

Captive Insurers

*E*arly *in my insurance career, in 1961, I became intrigued with alternatives to the conventional approach of paying premiums and buying insurance. One was an internal reserve and a second was the then-shocking idea of creating your own insurance company. Captive insurance companies grew from an isolated idea to a major movement. They continue to have significant advantages as well as disadvantages. Here is a 2002 paper that recounts the history of these mechanisms and some of their current problems.*

The Cost of a Soda?
(July 2002)

In the aftermath of 9/11 and the accumulated underwriting ills of the property/casualty insurance industry, commercial insurance buyers experienced radical price increases and reductions in both coverage and available limits. For many, these reactions were excessive and irrational, and buyers now actively seek alternatives to conventional insurance. One group, the Air Transport Association of America, representing 22 major U.S. airlines, formed a new group captive insurance company in Vermont, named Equitime. It will provide terrorism coverage to its members, who will contribute as much as US$50 million to capitalize the new venture. It will offer up to $300 million in protection, with $2 billion of excess support provided by the U.S. government.

How did the commercial insurance industry react to this commendable effort? Maurice R. (Hank) Greenberg, the chairman of the American

International Group (AIG), demands that the government end its reinsurance support of the new company. Let market forces work, he suggests. This is the same executive who rushed to Washington last fall with his fellow CEOs to plead for government reinsurance of the entire industry to the tune of 90% of all terrorism losses over $10 billion and a smaller percentage of the losses under $10 billion. He still supports this handout. He wants Uncle Sam to support his insurers but not a new competitor created by his customers.

As its option, AIG proposes to the airlines a terrorism insurance rate of $1.00 to $1.50 per passenger. Greenberg argues that any cost would be "passed through to the consumer and is hardly more than the cost of a soda." At over 100 million passengers per year, the airlines' cost would exceed $100 million—radically higher than what they propose to charge themselves through the captive. That's a pretty impressive soda! Is this how the marketplace should function, with the government supporting an inefficient and volatile insurance industry but not those who choose to create shared funding mechanisms? Chris Duncan, the CRO of Delta Airlines and principal architect of Equitime, responded to Greenberg's comment by saying, "It is enough to say that we have a difference of opinion of what a real, functioning marketplace is."

This kerfuffle reminds me of similar reactions, in previous insurance "crises." In the 1840s, when the underwriters at Lloyd's threatened New York ship-owners with radically higher insurance rates, the owners responded by creating their own marine insurance company, known as Atlantic Mutual, a company that evolved into a standard insurer and continues to this day. In the late 1800s, factory owners bristled when insurance companies would not give them credit for their newly-developed automatic sprinkler systems. They formed their own "factory mutuals," now merged into FM Global. In 1929, the Protestant Episcopal Church in the United States, with some help from J. P. Morgan, established the Church Insurance Company to underwrite its churches and related properties in the face of unrealistic premiums. Beginning in the late 1960s, many governmental entities created their own risk-sharing pools in response to distinct non-interest by regular insurers. I remember the agonized complaints of commercial insurers when a group of Connecticut municipalities formed the Connecticut Interlocal Risk Management

Agency. They moaned that CIRMA was under-funded, would attract only the worst towns and would be bust within a few years. Today it is the largest underwriter of governmental entities in the state. In the mid-1970s, when commercial insurers dumped their medical malpractice customers or demanded exorbitant rates (in one instance I know, an insurance company offered to provide $1 million in *aggregate* protection in one year for $1.3 million!), hospitals and doctors joined to create new captive insurance companies, derisively nicknamed "bedpan mutuals" by their commercial competitors. In the last insurance crisis of the mid-1980s, corporations, educational institutions and even nonprofits pooled their resources to build new insurers such as ACE, XL, SCUUL, and YMCA Mutual. All of these responses to unsettled times served their owners well and most continue operating today.

Tony Bridger, the risk manager of the Bank of Montreal, summarized the situation some years ago when he concluded, "Volatility can be managed; overreaction cannot." Captive insurers have consistently brought new capital, innovative ideas and fresh underwriting expertise to an industry that needs periodic external rejuvenation. Captives, in that sense, have been an important part of the functioning marketplace for more than 150 years.

What are captive insurance companies? How have they developed over the past 30 plus years? Do they really serve a legitimate purpose in today's economy? To answer these questions, I researched my own personal work with captives, drawing on four published articles.

1968   In 1968, the captive idea was in its infancy. I wrote a paper that year for *Business Insurance* (January 15, 1968), entitled "Putting the Captive Company in Perspective." I counted 200-300 captives owned by U.S. parents, operating in the United States and on offshore islands, with premiums in the vicinity of $400-$500 million. Most were single-parent entities, owned by a non-insurance corporation and underwriting only their parents' risks. A few were group captives, serving related organizations, such as the Belk Stores. Premiums paid to captives then were fully deductible. Most parents used their companies to fund higher property insurance deductibles and create what were effectively tax-deferred internal reserves. They were, I wrote, "the ultimate in self-insurance technique." I warned, however, that "tax regulations could easily change" and that contending that a captive could produce a profit was "sheer wishful thinking." I was entranced by the potential of this new medium.

1979   Eleven years later, doubts crept into my thinking. In "Captives in a Quandary," from the *Proceedings of the Third International Captive Insurance Company Conference—Bermuda* (March 1979), I reported that the U.S. Internal Revenue Service in the United States ruled that premiums paid to single parent captives were no longer deductible (Revenue Ruling 77-316). The IRS promptly won a pivotal lawsuit against the Carnation Company in December 1978. European tax authorities began to consider their own constricting rules. Wherever possible, other regulators threw up roadblocks. The rush of captives to Bermuda had also created a strain on its infrastructure: captives reportedly accounted for 14% of the islands' GNP. Yet interest continued. I counted almost 1,000 captives worldwide, with $4 to $5 billion in premiums alone for the U.S.-owned companies. The exploding medical malpractice crisis in the United States spawned numerous hospital and doctor-owned insurers, which, as a group, underwrote almost 20% of all U.S. hospital beds. I concluded: "The future of captives lies largely in the degree to which they can convince tax and regulatory authorities of their legitimacy, avoid ill-advised underwritings, create a firmer financial base, and complement the conventional world insurance market."

1987   After another nine years, I reviewed the captive scene again in *Business Insurance* (October 26, 1987), this time more optimistically under the title "Captives' Role in Industry to Increase." The count had more than doubled, to over 2,500 companies throughout the world. Captives were now a global phenomenon. By 1987, we were plunging down again in another market cycle in which insurers irrationally increased rates and withheld protection. I commented then that everything was in flux: the commercial marketplace, regulation, taxation and the law. I forecast—wrongly, as it turned out—that in five years we would have fewer, but substantially stronger, captives. I also forecast, more correctly, that Bermuda would become a "third market," that captives would expand to cover "unfundable" loss exposures such as environmental, earthquake and political risks, and that they would create liaisons with other financial markets. We needed, I suggested, new global regulations covering both captives and other insurance companies. This, unfortunately, has not happened, despite the Basel Committee's promising new guidelines for financial institution capital sufficiency.

1992   In my next commentary on captives, "Captive Insurers in the Key of C," (*RMR* April 1992), the total count had grown to 3,350 with an estimated $10 billion in capital and surplus. Captives continued to be formed, even in the midst of a renewed "soft" market, and owners and prospective owners still believed that they met the five criteria of cost-savings, coverage, cash flow, capacity and control. Yet I questioned their utility. Too many single parent captives were operated as "corporate toys," insurance playthings that "piddled with trivial (financial) issues." I argued that most failed "to respond to the real economic and risk challenges confronting their parent companies." They fell into the same trap that entangled commercial insurers: irrelevancy.

2002   Managers didn't listen to the grumblings of this cantankerous gadfly! Today, 4,500+ captive insurers operate around the world. They account for $50 billion in annual premiums, $202 billion in capital and surplus, and $230 billion in investable assets (all figures from the *Captive Insurance Company Directory, Captive Insurance Company Reports* and other sources). The crunch of a market out of control contributes to fresh consideration of self-insurance, single parent captives and especially group captives, such as Equitime and sEnergy, a business interruption and property pool created by twelve energy companies from the United States, Canada, South Africa, Denmark and Norway. Yet, despite the pressures of the times and the continuing enthusiasm for captives, more observers question their effectiveness.

Hugh Rosenbaum, the editor emeritus of *Captive Insurance Company Reports*, the quintessential monthly journal for the industry, wrote recently in *Emphasis* (No. 2, 2001): "For each argument in favor of a captive, there is a counter-argument for a better alternative." He suggests a new metric for assessing the relative value of a captive: comparison to the true alternatives—full insurance *and* non-insurance.

His qualms are echoed by an academic study, "Do Insurance Captives Enhance Shareholders' Value?" by Mike Adams and David Hillier, in *Risk Management: An International Journal* (Vol. 4, No. 2, 2002). Although their data are out-of-date (they use 1997 figures), their conclusions merit thought. They write, "The empirical evidence suggests that an investment in a captive insurance subsidiary is likely to turn out a zero-sum game for many public corporations, with managers winning at shareholders' expense. Insurance captives are often sold to corporate managers as risk management solutions without an in-depth and critical appraisal of how such solutions are expected to add value for shareholders. Many shareholders are likely to be better off by diversifying their risks through holding better-balanced portfolios of investments rather than by having their companies establishing captive insurers. Changes in the taxation code in many jurisdictions, including the United States and United Kingdom, have also reduced the financial flexibility and efficiency of the captive insurance concept as a risk management vehicle."

While I emphatically disagree about a focus only on shareholders to the exclusion of other "investors," the Rosenbaum and Adams-Hillier reservations suggest that we should consider other options. Add to these doubts other disturbing factors. In the aftermath of the Enron collapse and the Tyco and Stanley disclosures, many governments question the use of offshore, tax shelter vehicles such as "special purpose entities" (SPEs) and captives. New regulations are inevitable. Adverse publicity continues. Captives also now cost considerably more, with the rise of reinsurance costs (captives remain capitalized at relatively low levels and require much reinsurance) and the explosion of annual "fronting" costs, from around 5% to 15% or higher. "Fronting" is still necessary because of antiquated local regulations that require the use of "admitted" insurers—a form of protectionism that makes no sense in a global economy. Finally, add the flurry of news articles when Arthur Andersen's Bermuda captive announced that it would not cover a professional liability settlement because, as reported, the parent company had failed to pay its premiums!

If cracks now appear in the captive edifice, and the conventional market continues in erratic disarray, how can managers fund their risks? I offer six suggestions.

First, I suggest that the goal of risk financing must be to build and maintain reputation, the critical ingredient for organizational survival. Most quantifiable insurance "losses" seldom have a material effect on an organization. Maintaining a favorable perception on the part of customers, employees, suppliers, regulators, lenders and communities carries far more weight than recovering some dollars for fire damage or the expenses of a lawsuit. So, risk financing must be flexible and liquid so that managers have the funds necessary to reestablish credibility. Flexibility and efficiency are the keystones, as confirmed by Adams and Hillier.

Second, the critical idea for the future is building reserves for contingencies. These reserves can be internal or external. They can be concrete (an internal fund, or a line-of-credit) or qualitative (the willingness of shareholders and lenders to advance more funds in the event they are needed). They must also be flexible and easy to access. Slow recoveries or those restricted to certain contractual stipulations (see most insurance clauses) are useless.

Third, owners can and should consider radical increases in the capital of their captives, if they are to serve real financial needs. BP's Jupiter, domiciled in Guernsey, is capitalized at £1 billion ($1.4 billion). Postcap, the Consignia (United Kingdom's ex-Royal Mail, soon to be Royal Mail again!) captive, also in Guernsey, is capitalized at £100 million, although only £1 million is paid in. If a captive makes sense, why not put enough money into it to allow it to play a significant role in corporate affairs? Is this effective use of capital? If we measure results in terms of preservation of reputation following major contingencies, rather than looking more narrowly at return on equity, it probably is.

Fourth, regulations such at the U.S. Risk Retention Act can and should be expanded to permit captives to underwrite not only liability but also property and other insurance, with a minimum of restrictive state regulations. It's time to remove, in both the United States and elsewhere around the world, requirements that corporate insurance must be locally admitted. Here is where creation of global financial standards and regulation will spur more efficiency in risk financing.

Fifth, major corporations should lobby governments to permit new tax-deferred catastrophe reserves, reserves to which contributions are tax deductible and in which earned investment income is credited without taxation. Individuals in the United States are now permitted to build their pension funds in this fashion. These funds may also be used, in certain circumstances, to fund personal catastrophes. This idea would obviate the need for captives, onshore or offshore, since any corporation would have the same reserving capability of an insurance company. Michael Walters, a principal of Tillinghast-Towers Perrin, writes a challenging description of a "Tax-Deferred Catastrophe Account" in *Emphasis* (No. 2, 2002). Although his brief supports such an account for an insurance company (with which I agree), it should be equally applicable to any non-insurance organization. This idea comes laden with tax implications—a one-time tax deduction—but its long-term implications for the sustainability of organizations argues for serious review. It's high time that we dropped this insane idea of managing only for the next quarter.

Finally, risk financing should consider all forms of funding—from charges to current operating income and internal reserves (tax deductible or not) to external pooling (group captives), lines of credit, equity financing and use of capital markets. The increasing use of catastrophe bonds presages an entirely new approach to funding major contingencies. As these capital markets become more liquid, overhead costs will diminish and make them more competitive with other options. Remember that a cat bond is cash in hand. It must be invested and cannot be used until and unless the named contingency occurs, but it is immediately and fully available for use, in sharp distinction to most conventional insurance.

Hank Greenberg's characterization of the cost of conventional insurance as being nothing more than the "cost of a soda" is incomplete and incorrect. Conventional insurance has lost its fizz! His comment, however, forces us to take a fresh look at how we finance risk, from reserves, to captives, to insurance. It's time to put the bubbles back in risk financing.

CHAPTER 11

Catastrophes

Some unexpected outcomes are much worse than anticipated. A "disaster" or "catastrophe"—whether it affects but one organization, everyone in a region, or many globally—requires creativity and planning so that we can rebound from its effects. These are the events that sit at the tail of quantitative distributions, the 1% outliers that tend to be overlooked, simply because they happen infrequently or haven't happened at all before! They are the ultimate tests of risk management.

Toxic Chemicals
(May/June 1975)

The technology explosion of the past fifty years has created many new chemical compounds that, in our haste to apply for growth and profits, have not been properly tested for their ultimate effect on humans and the environment. We are beginning to learn what we have done to ourselves, perhaps sadly. The vinyl chloride situation is probably a forerunner of far more serious discoveries, affecting how our businesses are run.

Two current items emphasize this point. First is *Working Is Dangerous to Your Health*, written by Jeanne M. Stellman and Susan M. Daum. It's billed as a "handbook of health hazards in the workplace and what you can do about them." I can't think of another recent book so valuable to a risk manager in understanding some of the possible problems of injuries and deaths caused by dusts, noise, chemical, etc., all of which are largely work-related.

The second item is an article by Paul Brodheur in the April 7, 1975 issue of *The New Yorker*, on the potential damage to the ozone layer of the earth through the release of chlorofluorocarbons into the atmosphere from the ubiquitous aerosol can. Assuming a 10% increase in use to 1990 and level use thereafter, scientists predict a 5% to 7% destruction of the ozone layer by 1995, growing to as high as 30% to 50% by 2050. Since the presence of the ozone layer makes human life on earth possible, there is serious scientific concern about the continued use of aerosol propellants. The result of these predictions will be increased pressure for the passage of a Toxic Sunstances Control Act by Congress.

Bhopal: A Risk Management Trigger?
(November/December 1984)

The magnitude of the disaster at Bhopal is just beginning to emerge. The incredible loss of life, the thousands of injured, the potential after-effects of the chemical fog, and the disruption of lives will give rise to more and more probing questions. Is this the price to pay for technology? Do we know as much as we need to about the wide variety of chemical compounds used in industry? What levels of safety are "safe enough?" Is it possible to achieve the same standards of safety in both developed and less developed areas of the world? What level of public disclosure and regulatory control is required to prevent such disasters?

Other areas of concern focus on the survival of multinational companies in certain countries, the effect on the world insurance system, and, of course, on Union Carbide. Bhopal joins other names such as Love Canal, Minimata Bay, Flixborough, Three Mile Island and Seveso in the litany of hits and near misses as we try to come to grips with the problems of technology that may run wild. The National Academy of Sciences studied over 30,000 chemicals and concluded that *less than 10%* have verified, reliable information on their potential health hazards. We are dealing with an incredibly large unknown.

Although it is tragic that such a disaster is the spur, Bhopal is an opportunity to create a more effective and responsive risk assessment and risk response mechanism for American industry. For the past two decades we have been far too finance oriented, too concerned with short-term financial gains and losses, and too little concerned with the potential long-term effects of much of what we create and sell.

The tragedy in Bhopal can be an impetus for new procedures in risk assessment and in long-term benefit analyses. It could trigger a mandate for a more serious staff function in risk control, contingency planning, and crisis management. And it could help organizations to develop new mechanisms for financing responses. It won't happen overnight, but early 1985 can be the beginning. This evolution may well make it imperative as well as profitable to address seriously some of the risk assessment and risk control issues we've been avoiding.

Of Disasters, Catastrophes and Other Bad Things
(October 1994)

What is a "disaster," a "catastrophe"? The Swiss Reinsurance Company defines a disaster as "20 deaths, 2000 made homeless, or a total damage loss of US$57 million." Bill McGannon, Nova Chemical's Risk Manager, defines a catastrophe as "a loss equal to 1.5 times annual profit and/or including one or more serious injuries or deaths to employees." Whether a definition includes a finite number of deaths, injuries or dollars of loss, or is more related to organization size, we can all agree that it is an event that hits us hard. Most of us, thankfully, have never had to face a true disaster. Those of us who have know that it is truly the challenge of a career. Disasters and catastrophes are precisely what risk managers are employed to assess, avoid, control or otherwise finance.

Understanding the nature of potential disaster is a continuing responsibility of a risk manager. In 1991-92 alone, the global economic losses from natural disasters were over US$100 billion. It is the focus of an ambitious ten-year program of the United Nations, called the International Decade for Natural Disaster Reduction (IDNDR). This past May, IDNDR held a major symposium in Yokohama to explore progress since the start of the decade and to develop principles to guide work up to the year 2000. Representatives of 147 states attended, plus members of regional, national and local organizations and the private sector. To most of us, the opening statement of Dr. Olavi Elo seems painfully obvious: "Today, the reasons for having created the Decade may appear to be somewhat trite: mankind seems to have stumbled into a proliferation of political, ethnic and religious upheavals . . . Societies are so overwhelmed by human emergencies, by human disasters, that we have halted in our tracks, as it were, on the road to progress and development, to stand helplessly by, paralyzed, watching so many human tragedies unravel before our eyes." Equally obvious is the conclusion that relief alone cannot overcome a disaster. IDNDR is therefore developing a global program of fresh approaches to disaster management, information collection, communication, and, above all, coordinated international prevention, preparedness and mitigation.

IDNDR has undertaken over 30 special projects worldwide. It reports on its work in *Stop Disasters*, a bimonthly newsletter. It intends to share information on the Internet in the future. More than 48 conferences have been scheduled through 1996, eight in the United States. The Yokohama Conference concluded with a worldwide appeal to create new partnerships to "build a safer world, based on common interest, sovereign equality, and shared responsibility to save human lives, (and) protect human and natural resources, the ecosystem, and cultural heritage."

The principles set forth at this conference are familiar to risk managers:

- Risk assessment is a necessary step for the adoption of adequate and successful disaster reduction policies and measures.
- Disaster reduction and preparedness are of primary importance.
- Disaster prevention and preparedness must be considered integral aspects of development policy.
- Prevention, reduction and mitigation are disaster priorities.
- Early warnings are key factors for prevention and preparedness.
- Preventive measures must involve participation at all levels.
- Vulnerability can be reduced by proper design and development patterns.
- The international community must share disaster control technology.
- Environmental protection is essential to the program.
- Each country bears primary responsibility, supported by the international community.

In a paper I wrote entitled "Considering Catastrophes," (*RMR* October 1993), I noted the rising concern of many risk managers that conventional insurance might be inadequate to meet the challenge of funding catastrophes. Others agree. Frank Nutter, the president of the Reinsurance Association of America, in the August 1994 issue of *Best's Review*, supported the enactment of the pending Natural Disaster Protection Act (NDPA) by Congress. Under NDPA, the Federal Government and the Federal Emergency Management Agency would provide reinsurance to insurers and sponsor mitigation efforts at the state level.

New Zealander Shaun Wilkinson, retired risk manager for Fletcher Challenge, sees group pools and governmental and regional arrangements as the ultimate financial resources for catastrophes: "We are seeing the response capability of the insurance industry shrinking day by day for a number of reasons. In the past the industry has not employed particularly sophisticated risk assessment skills. Furthermore in general terms, the industry worldwide tends to be inadequately capitalized, with many companies under-reserved by at least 20%. At the same time attempts by the insurance industry to develop new funding mechanisms, such as finite risk insurance or financial reinsurance, are attacked by the accounting profession, which seems to be more interested in full disclosure to investors than in ensuring adequate underwriter solvency and thereby adequate protection for policyholders. Regulators in many countries are increasingly trying to act like underwriters by determining what rates and policy terms insurers should charge. Governments, in an attempt to collect taxes earlier, are preventing the insurance industry from creating viable catastrophe reserves. The net result is that we have already reached the limits of insurability for such exposures as earthquake, windstorm, and flood. It is a regrettable fact that corporate insurance buyers can no longer rely on the insurance or the reinsurance industry to help them transfer those losses that could seriously affect their organizations' long-term existence. They are therefore forced to look for alternatives."

If indeed the private sector alone cannot meet the risk financing challenge, some of the alternatives may be the developing regional and international organizations that have been predicted by the IDNDR. A joint private and public sector initiative may be the answer for many trans-national organizations. This means that risk managers should become active participants in the work of IDNDR so that they can help shape the solutions.

Gray Tuesday
(November 1994)

It was a brisk, clear, altogether pleasant autumn day in Connecticut, but the world news on Tuesday, October 4, brought two items of serious concern to me and to risk managers. The first was the massive earthquake off the Kurile Islands, north of Japan. While the reported damage and loss of life have been minimal, the size of the quake—7.9 on the Richter scale—was about the same as the Great Kanto quake of 1923 that wreaked havoc in Tokyo and killed 140,000 people. With an epicenter closer to central Japan, a comparable earthquake could cause *insured* losses in excess of US$800 billion! That's not a typo—it's a recent estimate from a Stanford University professor and a consulting firm in Palo Alto, California. Japanese insurers, heavy investors in U.S. Treasury bills, would be forced to liquidate their investments, causing global financial market repercussions. The reinsurance market could be shattered. It hasn't happened yet, but the severity of the October quake is a clear warning.

The second shock was no less significant. A British High Court judge ruled in favor of Lloyds "names" (investors in syndicates) who had sued their agents and underwriters over the bankruptcy of the Gooda Walker syndicate, alleging negligence. The settlement may reach some US$790.7 million. It is the largest civil judgment in English history. Moreover, it could be a precedent for the other names who are suing their agents and syndicates. Until these cases are resolved, the on-going financial condition of the Lloyd's market remains in serious question. The omens are not good.

The events of Gray Tuesday remind us that even the strongest financial institutions are susceptible to collapse, directly or indirectly. They reemphasize the fragility of global systems used for risk financing.

Holy Cow!
(May 1996)

It is a classic example of risk mismanagement. I'm referring to the bovine spongiform encephalopathy (BSE)—"mad cow"—scare that surfaced in Great Britain in mid-March, just when I happened to be in London. The EU banned British beef. The "beefeaters" reluctantly flocked to chickens and fish. The Conservative government dithered and dallied, reinforcing the public's lack of confidence in government's ability to understand the degree of risk, much less solve it. Wild solutions surfaced. Some Cambodians suggested that English cows be shipped to that country where they could be used to help explode still buried landmines. Still others proposed sending 4.6 million cattle to India where the Hindus revere rather than eat them. *The Economist* indulged in its normal quota of punning headlines for the story: "Silence of the Calves," and "Cowed."

Scientific research indicates a possible linkage between BSE, a fatal disease to cattle, and a human counterpart, Creutzfeldt-Jakob disease (CJD), but the connection remains unproved. A new strain of CJD (variant CJD) has been identified in England in about 12 recent cases among younger people from farming communities, but a cross-species infection is still doubtful. BSE, which scientists believe is related to scrapie in sheep, has existed for centuries. Why hasn't there been previous evidence of transmittal to humans?

While scientists ponder these questions, politicians and business people must take action. It is a classic situation of managing risk, which hinges on the critical element of the public's perception of that risk.

Following an earlier outbreak of BSE in 1989, the British government then argued that British beef was perfectly safe and made a decision to ban the mixture of beef offal in cattle feed, and finally procrastinated when the possible connection to CJD surfaced earlier this year. Other organizations quickly recognized the risk implications and took immediate responsive action. McDonald's—within days of the new announcement—dropped all English beef from its 660 outlets in Britain, replacing it with chicken, fish and vegetarian burgers, and later with beef from safe sources. It took out full-page ads in English papers. It wasn't a question about the relatively remote risk of contracting CJD, judged to be about the same as winning the lottery, but about public perception and what an adverse reaction could do to both income and reputation.

McDonald's contingency planning is an example to both governments and other corporations. Competitive chains delayed and may have lost some market share as a result.

All of this has re-focused attention on the question of the relative riskiness of various products and the reactions to new problem areas. We face a continuing battle among the scientific "experts," many of whom disagree, government regulators charged with protecting the public and the public whose perceptions are so easily influenced by the press. How and when should an organization respond to a new crisis? The BSE affair shows that rebuilding and maintaining public confidence, particularly in consumer products, probably takes precedence over other considerations, ranging from this quarter's earnings per share to re-election prospects.

Saying that, we must recognize the potential for future unintended consequences. Mass panic is contagious, requiring swift and recognizable action, so beware of the results of those actions. Woodrow Wyatt, writing in *The Times* (London) on March 26, 1996, at the height of the crisis, argued that the "herd instinct" be resisted, since life consists of risk. "Flight from risk is a fantasy," he suggested. It would be impossible to eliminate, for example, the 3,650 road deaths each year in Britain and the 18,000 deaths from influenza. His coldly rational conclusion about BSE and a possible CJD connection: "The disease may be horrible for the sufferers and their relatives, but the risk is too small to justify the destruction of the cattle industry." I disagree, for this same industry is just as quickly destroyed if consumers in Britain and abroad decide to forego English beef or are prevented by regulators from consuming it.

I agree with Mr. Wyatt's warning about possible new risk consequences: "Banning marginally risky products frequently has unintended consequences. The late Lord Rothschild, in his remarkable lecture, 'Risk' in 1978, cited the banning of DDT by Sri Lanka in the early 1960s, induced by an emotional book, *Silent Spring,* by Rachel Carson. Sri Lanka endured a virulent epidemic of malaria spread by mosquitoes, which could have been eliminated by DDT."

Using the BSE situation as an example, risk managers should understand the importance of the public's perception of risk, the volatility of that perception, the need for rapid contingency responses, *and* the possibility that unintended consequences may occur.

La Vache Qui Risqué
(February 1997)

The announcement in the House of Commons last March that ten new cases of variant Creutzfeldt-Jakob Disease (vCJD) had been discovered in Great Britain and that they might be related to B.S.E. (bovine spongiform encephalopathy), or "mad cow" disease, set off an uproar that has yet to subside. I first commented on this situation in the May 1996 *RMR* ("Holy Cow!") It continues to be a perfect example of the mismatch between instant global communications and our imperfect knowledge. The first reaction was to swear off British beef, and the European Union still maintains this ban. Yet, as an incisive article by John Lanchester in *The New Yorker* (Dec. 2, 1996) argues, the presumed sources of the contagion—the rendered parts of a slaughtered cow (brain, spinal cord, etc.), reformulated as feed for cattle—also go into many other products such as gelatin (used in candies, mayonnaise, lipstick, and ice cream), collagen (used in sausage casing and glue), tallow and fat (used in soap, detergent, linoleum, insecticide and margarine), and keratin (used in shampoo). In a modern interdependent economy, nothing is wasted and therefore the potential for infection may be that much greater.

The key is whether or not a long-known animal disease (known as scrapie in sheep) can cross to the human species. The Lanchester paper suggests three scenarios. One, there may be no connection between B.S.E. and the new variant of CJD, despite a growing consensus on such a linkage. Two, the species barrier may not exist at all, and, within a five year incubation period, we may uncover hundreds of thousands of people with fatal brain disease, a "disaster of Old Testament proportions" as Lanchester calls it. Or three, the connection may exist but the species barrier may limit the disease to only a few. This is the most likely scenario according to the recent research.

For the practicing risk manager, the unknowns greatly outweigh the knowns. If you run a cafeteria in England, should you serve beef? But aren't the risks (so far) relatively minuscule when compared to the accidents arising from the use of company automobiles by employees? As with all risks, we have to make decisions based not only on the most recent expert assessments of frequency and severity potentials, but also on the public's rapidly-changing perceptions, often easily twisted by the revelations of the press.

The Moment of Truth
(November 2000)

Being a serious student of risk management, I experienced some qualms during my last visit to San Francisco, the city of light and jiggles. The evening was uncharacteristically warm—a record 108 degrees F. had been recorded that afternoon over in East Bay—as we settled into our seats at the Opera House for Luisa Miller, Verdi's tragic drama that ends with two poisonings and a shooting. Late in the first act, the hero, taken with an avowal of love by the heroine, sings, "the earth trembles at my feet." I braced myself for the inevitable. Fortunately the San Andreas Fault remained quiet, untempted by this felicitous opportunity to make mortals quake. My companion reminded me that it was just such an evening eleven years earlier, also in the fall following a heat wave, when the Loma Prieta earthquake rumbled through the Bay Area. The moment passed and, with relief, we later slipped out into the cool evening air, refreshed by Verdi and gratified that the temptation of fate in the Opera House did not cause a convulsion.

> . . . the more emotionally fraught an event or phenomenon is,
> the more eagerly people search for a story to make sense of it.
> **John Allen Paulos, *Once Upon a Number*,**
> **Basic Books, New York 1998**

September 11, 2001
(October 2001)

It was unspeakable and unexpected, but not unimaginable. I had just started to read my morning emails when I received a note from one daughter telling me than another, who works in lower Manhattan, was safe. It was 9:20 A.M. Confused, I immediately turned on the television to see and hear the chaos, first at the World Trade Center and then in Washington. Throughout that day and the next few days I experienced the same outrage, shock, anger, horror and compassion for all those affected, and a growing numbness that millions around the world also felt.

I was eight years old when Pearl Harbor was bombed and my memory is of an ashen-faced father listening at home in Philadelphia to the news reports and to President Roosevelt's address to Congress. The vaunted insularity of the United States was shattered. I was twenty-nine on that November 22 when word came from Dallas about the death of John F. Kennedy. We gathered around a portable radio in an 8th floor office in the Public Ledger Building, in Philadelphia, wondering how we as a country could survive. Now September 11 is the third in my personal litany of world-shaking events, viewed this time from Tenants Harbor, Maine.

This day is a solemn warning of our mutual vulnerability to the insane, the irrational and the fanatic—especially in a more closely-linked world interested in increased, not fewer, personal freedoms in travel, work, and expression. It is a reminder of the heroism and selflessness of our emergency services. It will also be a symbol of the natural resilience of the people of New York, Washington and this entire country.

September 11 is a reminder of the burden of global power and our responsibility for using it wisely. We idealistically try to help those in need and those who cry out for political freedom, sometimes failing. We inevitably create resentment, some of which becomes a fanatical backlash. Yes, swift and sure retribution is required, but we must also reach out to communicate with those who disagree, trying to understand their views just as we teach ours. This outreach is a long-term effort, needed especially in the Muslim world. From vulnerability must come resilience, a refreshed respect for the views of others, and a renewed confidence in ourselves, in our future and in our ideals. Adversity in this case breeds renewed strength, commitment and unity.

A return to some form of normalcy is the best antidote to this disaster but will we ever again board a plane or take an elevator in a high-rise building without a twinge of memory for September 11, 2001?

A Letter to My Readers
(September 2004)

> . . . they wait for the moments during which life counts. When
> they arrive, these moments, they come and pass quickly.
> Afterwards, nothing is quite the same and they wait once more.
>
> **John Berger, *To The Wedding*,**
> **Vintage International, New York 1996**

It's been three years since September 11, 2001, forever enshrined as *9/11,* and six months since March 11, 2004, the train bombing in Madrid. After these events, nothing *is* quite the same. Those of us who deal daily with the management of risk face new uncertainties and the need to construct new responses. This is a personal commentary, my observations on how we have changed post 9/11. As more than half of my readers live outside the United States, it is also a candid appraisal of the actions of this country.

9/11 and its subsequent events crushed the euphoria surrounding the demise of communism. In our innocence we thought that we had embarked on a long period of peace, freedom, and economic advancement for everyone, one in which the overwhelming military power of one country would support this advance and throttle the petty ambitions of minor tyrants. That innocence is gone, replaced by two cancerous growths that increase uncertainty and threaten global stability. One is a mounting antipathy to the United States and everything it stands for. The other is a loss of trust in institutions, public and private. How the world reacts to these two challenges will dictate the course of history in the next two to three decades.

First, the growing antipathy to the United States and its culture is based on both recent actions and lack of action. This country is accused of acting preemptively and unilaterally, without global support, and acting precipitously, without adequate information or intelligence. We also stand accused of failing to act where conditions otherwise warrant action. These are fair accusations but they must be considered in the circumstances of the times. Leaders, like executives and risk managers, must make decisions under uncertainty, collecting available data but always being pressed by time and conditions to act. Did Al Qaeda have further acts of terrorism in the works after 9/11? Would others extremists follow suit, perhaps with weapons far more damaging than four aircraft? Would others be emboldened by Al Qaeda's success to attempt similar acts of terrorism? In its prompt and powerful responses in both Afghanistan and Iraq, the United States crushed two obnoxious regimes, but, in so doing, it also risked raising the specter of an arrogant and abrasive super-power acting arbitrarily anywhere in the world where it thought that its interests were being challenged, and, in an ironic twist, it probably increased the animosity of those prone to terrorist acts.

At the same time as the world recoiled at what it believed to be an excessive use of power, it began to find flaws in the economics, culture and politics of the United States. The United States, they pointed out, is the home of excess. It compensates private-sector executives excessively, far beyond levels elsewhere in the world. It tolerates an excessive indulgence in drugs. While the United States tries, on one hand, to exterminate the production of heroin, cocaine and marijuana at home and abroad, it permits and encourages unprecedented pill-taking for every conceivable symptom or illness, real or imagined. It is a drug-saturated society. Its citizens also eat to excess, making obesity the country's primary physical impairment. It indulges in excessive litigation, permitting an unrestrained plaintiffs' bar to obtain individual and class action judgments far beyond the wildest imagination or rational compensation. And, yes, it is also justifiably accused of entertainment characterized by excessive ugliness, distortion and commercialism. Is there anything that isn't for sale?

The economic excess of the United States puts all the others to shame. When 9/11 should have forced fiscal prudence in light of the long-terms costs of battling terrorism, the United States plunged into economic gluttony: Congress cut taxes, increased spending and postponed the inevitable day of reckoning from its unfunded liabilities for social security and medical benefits. From a fiscal surplus at the end of the last century, it now has a skyrocketing deficit. It continues to try and finance this insatiable greed by asking investors abroad to buy its debt. It is a country beset by problems similar to other developed nations—an aging population and radical terrorism—but its reaction has, so far, been one exactly contrary to expert economic opinion.

Should the United States be judged only on the basis of this excess and on its recent activities around the world? Isn't it time to consider the native reservoir of prudence, caution and common sense that have characterized this nation for more than two centuries? Shouldn't we consider the freedoms of speech, political activism, and religion, and the availability of economic opportunity, and its culture of innovation, all of which have blessed its inhabitants for so long? Shouldn't we also consider its uncommon history of recoiling from excess when its people realize the costs and effects?

The recent criticism is warranted in many areas, but this country is listening. I remain optimistic that we can and will change the current run of excess.

The second outgrowth of 9/11 is more serious, as it reflects a global problem: the loss of trust in institutions and the erosion of credibility in those who lead.

When I hear a politician or business executive pontificating, I immediately recoil at the words "the fact of the matter is . . ." This is a preface to mendacity, a shovel full of slanted if not incorrect information. The bursting of the stock market bubble and the aftermath of 9/11 jointly demolished our trust in elected officials, in election processes, in the word of leaders, in the published reports of corporations and their auditors, and in our long-standing faith in the efficacy of markets. Lack of candor and the inability to apologize, to admit fault, are the prevailing winds. Politicians and executives are afraid to admit error for fear of being ousted from office. Both are driven by fear of their constituents. Peter Bernstein pointed out last month, "Nor will the data (quarterly corporate earnings numbers) ever attain credibility as long as investors require CEOs to perform high-wire pirouettes every three months in an effort to make the earnings numbers come out where investors hope they will be, and to dream up persuasive excuses for shortfalls." (*Economics and Portfolio Strategy*, August 1, 2004) Are we afraid to face the truth?

A byproduct of this slippage in trust and credibility is the growing erosion in the pluralism and secularism that have been identified with the United States for so many years. The United States is beginning to castigate anyone who does not match the profile of a "safe" citizen. It is starting to rethink its century-old open borders for immigration. Some are arguing that English, and English alone, should be the national language. As we grow to distrust our neighbors, leaders and institutions, some revert to those who promise all the answers, substituting dogma for doubt and difficult answers. As Philip Gourevitch of *The New York Times* wrote on July 20, "Dogma is impervious to reality." It begins to breed a new and disturbing messianic group belief of our own righteousness, an ironic mirror to the equally antithetical belief of those we now oppose.

The growing antipathy to all things American and the loss of trust in the "system" are two outgrowths of the 9/11 disaster and its subsequent reactions. They will, I suspect, be with us for some time to come, but I believe they are temporary. The cures for these cancers continue to be honesty, candor and expanded communication with those who offer criticism. These three traits are, or should be, the natural tools of those who purport to manage risk. Why shouldn't we take the lead in this period of global uncertainty?

After writing these words, my editor, cook and constant companion noted sarcastically "Your soapbox is high enough to do Olympic back-flips. Were you robbed of a medal at Athens?" She brought me thumping to the ground!

> *Our concern with history . . . is a concern with preformed images already imprinted on our brains, images at which we keep staring while the truth lies elsewhere, away from it all, somewhere as yet undiscovered.*

W. G. Sebald, *Austerlitz* Modern Library, New York 2001

Charley, Frances, Ivan and Jeanne
(October 2004)

These four hurricanes of 2004, ones that lacerated the Caribbean and the southeast United States, remind me that natural disasters continue to defy rational response. As risk managers we have over 100 years of records of occurrences of floods, earthquakes, typhoons, cyclones, hurricanes, tornados, tsunamis and similar "natural" events. Our predictive abilities have improved dramatically during this century, radically reducing death tolls, at least in the more economically developed societies, even while the economic damage has sky-rocketed. Why is this? Perversely, many people move to wind and earthquake-prone regions in the belief that, first, it won't happen to them, and second, even if it does, "government" will bail them out with financial awards. The result is that the many (taxpayers in general and those who contribute to charitable relief organizations), end up subsidizing continued folly. Yes, many of the more responsible carry insurance, but even then, other policyholders serve as co-payers of their losses through increased premiums. Insurance itself covers only a modest portion of total losses. According to Munich Reinsurance Company, in 2002, the world sustained $55 billion in total damages from some 500 "natural disasters." Less than 25%, or $13 billion was insured, leaving the remainder to be borne by victims and society.

Howard Kunreuther, at the University of Pennsylvania's Risk Management & Decision Processes Center, a part of its Wharton School, continues to be a vocal advocate of a more sensible approach to reducing these disasters' economic carnage. It isn't enough to enact strict land use planning and building codes that apply to both existing and new structures. He argues that a combination of financial incentives and penalties must be used to change behaviors. The scattered wreckage of mobile homes in this year's hurricanes in the southern United States is testimony to the lack of political will to enforce rational responses. The states, the federal government and the private sector (banks, mortgage companies and insurance companies alike) are complicit in their unwillingness and inability to adopt sensible solutions experts have recommended for years. In the latest issue of the Center's *Risk Management Review* (http://opim.wharton.upenn.edu.risk), Professor Kunreuther again argues that enhanced land use and building codes must be enforced with rigor, supported by financial rewards and penalties. Mortgage sellers must *require* that homes and businesses meet state standards *before* granting loans. Similarly, insurance companies must *refuse* to underwrite structures without proper wind reinforcements or when they are sited in a flood plain, leaving their owners to bear the entire financial burden of their improvident behavior. And, most importantly, disaster funding from state and local governments *must not be offered* to those who failed to meet standards and who subsequently sustained losses from major events. This last mandate, however, runs counter to the natural instincts of politicians whose sole purpose is re-election. In any election year, the public coffers are opened, especially in critical swing states such as Florida. Professor Kunreuther acknowledges these problems, but he has some smart suggestions for anticipating the next disaster. Instead of requiring homeowners and business-owners to ante up the relatively high costs of retrofitting their buildings with current dollars or short-term borrowing, he proposes that such costs be folded into existing mortgages, thus spreading them over many more years and reducing immediate pain. That's a financial incentive worth considering, something supportable by other taxpayers. Some tax deductibility for a portion of these expenses is another option.

The problem, of course, is that all this sensible advice requires close coordination among local, state and federal governments as well as among banks, mortgage companies, insurers, and reinsurers, something that has not happened yet. It may be too much to ask, yet I applaud Professor Kunreuther for his ongoing efforts to change the status quo.

Reducing both death and economic losses has also been the goal of the United Nations International Strategy for Disaster Reduction (ISDR) (www.unisdr.org), the successor to its successful International Decade for Disaster Reduction, carried out from 1990 through 1999. Its focus is the monumental loss that occurs annually in the less developed world, where the vulnerability of people and societies is dramatic. As ISDR reports in its latest publication (*Living with Risk: A Global Review of Disaster Reduction Initiatives*, United Nations, Geneva 2004: see www.un.org/Pubs/sales.htm), the developing world has the highest population growth (70 to 80 million per year) coupled with the "smallest share of resources and the biggest burden of exposure to disasters." Its conclusion is "that risk reduction and disaster preparedness always make better economic sense that reliance on disaster relief." It recommends a combination of public debate, education and economic support, efforts that will have a material effect on the loss of life and property. It is a monumental tome, some 430 pages in the basic text, plus another 126 in appendices, but it should be invaluable for any organization that operates extensively in the developing world. Are you now outsourcing to India? Do you depend on parts or assembly from Southeast Asia, China and Central America? If so, you should be aware of the effects there of natural disasters and the means, outlined in this book, for more intelligent anticipation and response. In particular, the Annexes include a 57 page directory of international, national, regional and specialized organizations (with email addresses) involved with disaster reduction and related issue, invaluable should a risk manager seek assistance for an organization's operations in specific countries.

Charley, Frances, Ivan and Jeanne again remind us of the importance of planning in anticipation of predictable natural disasters.

> *This review . . . is about how we can continue to develop a culture of prevention. It is a voyage of both discovery and rediscovery, about how human decisions increase or reduce vulnerability to natural hazards. It explores the way in which the understanding of disaster management and risk has evolved over recent years.*
>
> **Living with Risk, United Nations, Geneva 2004**

Sumatra Tsunami
(January 2005)

The enormity of the December 26 tsunami is almost beyond belief. An undersea earthquake measuring 9.0 on the Richter Scale, whose tidal wave engulfed the shores of Indonesia, Malaysia, Myanmar, Thailand, Sri Lanka, Bangladesh, India, the Maldives and numerous small islands, leaves more than 100,000 dead (as of this writing), hundreds of thousands injured and millions displaced. According to the United Nations it was the fourth largest earthquake in recorded history. The subsequent health and economic effects in Southeast Asia are frightening to contemplate, as they include cholera and diarrhea from polluted drinking water. The world, under the leadership of the United Nations, is mounting an unprecedented relief effort.

This is the major risk management effort of 2005. The forthcoming meeting this month in Kobe, Japan, of the United Nation's International Strategy for Disaster Reduction (ISDR), about which I've written in *RMR* (March 2004), will focus on early warning systems, evacuation planning, and disaster resilience, all critical issues for risk managers. Keep in touch with the work of the ISDR via www.unisdr.org.

CHAPTER 12

Words

*A*s *I stated at the outset of this collection of essays, I've always been fascinated with words and their meanings. I've been a loyal and fascinated reader of William Safire's weekly columns in The New York Times, defining and dissecting words. So it is only natural that some of my pieces are more focused on words than on the management of risk. Here are a few, concluding with an exercise on clichés.*

The Law and the Profits
(February 1996)

I've have repeated some personal observations so often that they have assumed the mantle of dogma, at least in my mind. They are now "laws" from which I cannot escape. It may be time, therefore, to recap *Kloman's Law* and its two corollaries.

The *Law*, offered to a group of insurance brokers in 1971, is that *"Insurance is nothing but a prefunded line of credit."* Over time, we can agree that premiums must equal or exceed losses for any insurance mechanism to succeed. An insurance company acts as a depository for premiums (the pre-funding of losses) and disburses these funds as losses occur. For individuals and smaller firms, premiums will equal or exceed losses over the long-term, defined as 50 years or more. For the larger organization, the time span is much shorter, making it economic for these firms to assume greater proportions of their own risks and losses. The insurer acts as a fiduciary in holding and managing prudently the funds given to it, much as a bank operates. Its profits come from investment income of the funds at its disposal. An analysis of insurer net income for the past twenty years in the United States shows this to be true.

I developed the First Corollary to *Kloman's Law* in 1985: *"There is no such thing as risk transfer; there is only risk sharing."* An insurance company effectively operates as the coordinator of the shared risk by many disparate individuals and organizations. It pools the funds of the many for the losses of the few. This Corollary recognizes that the inherent risk remains the responsibility of the organization (or individual) even when some of its potential financial effects are shared with others. Insurance becomes a successful mechanism when the idea of partnership is ingrained in the relationship. The purest form of insurance is thus the reciprocal or the mutual, where each participant accepts and shares risk for all the others. While some cynics argue that mutual insurers are in business solely for the aggrandizement of their executive officers, many operate with this sharing principle paramount. These are the most successful mutuals in both insurance and risk management.

My Second Corollary is the most recent, developed in 1994: *"Counterparties are critical."* If insurance is akin to credit, and risk sharing is an essential attribute, then the financial condition of this "partner" is the most critical consideration: not price, services, or policy conditions. Any risk sharing partnership demands that each party understand and accept the financial condition of the other. The primary responsibility of any insurer is its ability to meet future commitments. Too many buyers fail to respect this Corollary in their haste to get the best deal.

Kloman's Law and its two corollaries help managers to recognize the economic realities in risk financing.

Bumpf and Kerfuffle
(June 1998)

Assaulted by a barrage of press releases, descending on me in the mail, in curled fax sheets and by telephone, I recall those delicious English words "bumpf" and "kerfuffle." My London lexicographer, Hugh Rosenbaum, defines "bumpf" as "miscellaneous, useless leaflets, official papers or documents." I extend it to include useless words and euphemisms, which seem to abound in this season of spring conferences and seminars, as flacks outdo one another in flowery client praise, encouraging us to visit their booths or hospitality suites, or listen to their executives postulate profundities. This deluge sinks me into a depressing "kerfuffle"—a fuss, commotion and agitation. So it's time for a curmudgeonly counter-attack on the mounds of bumpf that I recycle weekly. Most of it should be burned outright.

First, to the press releases. Every third phrase refers to "strategic alliances," "unsurpassed services," "unique products," "world-renowned engineering," and "global networks." Is there no humility left? Doesn't anyone even acknowledge that competitors exist? Oh, for a bit of candor! By failing to admit the obvious, company puffery is recycled even before it is opened.

Second, to words of bumpf. I will overlook my Copy Editor's constant harping on elimination of unnecessary adverbs (they are really, quite seriously useful) and making all sentences active, not passive. She's right. What raises my kerfuffle are the trite words and phrases that pass for original thought. If I see "value added" once more, I'll gag. If what I do adds nothing to your treasure, at least it adds to mine in the form of higher income. The pious posturing around the phrase "value added" adds no value, Q.E.D. And what of complaints about "the level playing field?" What the writer wants is to cut the competition off at the knees. Or "the bottom line." This abomination comes from the profound misconception that everything can be reduced to a numerical quantity—in dollars, euros or yen—something that the green-eye-shade bean counters have tried to foist on us for years. They are succeeding. Equally reprehensible (and unintelligible) are those useless words "core competencies," "empowerment," and "right-sizing,"—academic business-speak, respectively, for ability, authority and firing. Have we allowed military euphemisms to creep unmolested into our language? I regret that the word "stakeholders" may also belong in this pantheon of avoidables, as I am guilty of its overuse. It means those to whom an organization bears some responsibility. In carping against an over-focus on "shareholders," the investors who actually put up the money for an enterprise, I have slipped into excessive usage of the broader term. I can't think of a short and pithy substitute, however, so you may see "stakeholder" used again in these pages. It is a piece of jargon, but it is one that is a short-hand to understanding, rather than a wet blanket submerging the mind.

My last candidate for the Bumpf Hall of Fame is the warning phrase, "the fact of the matter is . . ." or "as a matter of fact." These words, favorites of politicians, always precede a highly biased opinion that should be subject to the highest degree of skepticism.

There, I feel better already. The bumpf pile is lower and my kerfuffle has subsided a bit.

Groaners
(July 2000)

I have eight chronic complaints, familiar to many readers. They elicit an audible groan when I hear or see them. They are, in no particular order:

1) **"Attitude"** One cannot have "attitude." This word requires, indeed demands, an adjective (cavalier, pugnacious, flippant, serious). Standing alone, without a modifier, the word means nothing and is useless.

2) **"Get-go"** Another slang expression better served by a single syllable (start) or several (beginning). I presume it is some fall-out from the race referee's "on your marks; get set; go."

3) **"As a matter of fact"** I've railed on this one before. It is particularly galling, especially when uttered by a politician. It really means that what you are about to hear is so slanted and corrupted that it is totally unreliable. The speaker is trying for a put-down but generally only succeeds in a put-out.

4) **"Closure"** Simply over-used. Try agreement, finish, THE END!

5) **Split infinitives** I know, I know, such oracles as William Safire, H. W. Fowler, and his successor editors permit infinitives to be split on occasion, but they grate on my ear and I will resist them to my demise. It seems that writers today take special delight in foisting these enormities on the reading public.

6) **"Data"** According to Webster's Dictionary of English Usage, "the word *data* is a queer fish." How true! Singularly, the Latin word is datum, hardly ever used today. Data, as a plural word, requires a plural verb.

7) **Introductions** What ever happened to last names? We seem to have slipped into an informal familiarity of first-name-only introductions that guarantee greater anonymity. Like the old crock that I am, I frequently interrupt with a request for last names (and perhaps a short personal history!) I almost prefer the Germanic habit of using only the last name, something that I endured for four years in boarding school, where masters commonly referred to you only by surname. That habit still persists. When I receive a telephone call asking for "Kloman," I know immediately that it's one of my school buddies.

8) **"It" and "They"** I refer to an organization in the singular in successive references. It is always "it," not "they," even if the title is The New York Mets, as I refer to the team, not the individuals. "It" and "they" are too often mixed, again jarring the listening ear. The English try this confusion right within a sentence, such as "Manchester United are a powerful team," convincing me yet again that we were absolutely right to break away from such archaisms over 200 years ago.

"Robust"
(January 1996)

What is it with this word, "robust," popping up fad-like in all forms of usage? Actuaries now refer to their "robust" numbers. President Clinton refers to "robust rules of engagement" for Bosnian troops. Advertisements refer to "robust" clothing. "Full of health and strength, vigorous," says my American Heritage Dictionary in definition, "powerfully built, sturdy, suited to physical strength or endurance." Yet there is also a secondary definition: "rough or crude; boisterous." I wonder if that is what the actuaries or the President intended? H. W. Fowler (*Modern English Usage*) notes that the prevailing 17th century usage was "robustious" with an emphasis on the "rough" or "crude" meaning. Is this a robust attempt at humor?

Latin Phrases
(January 1996)

Numquam periclum sine periclo vincitur. (A risk is never overcome except through risk.)
from Publius Syrus, (in 13 A.D)

Felix qui potuit rerum cognoscera causus. (Happiness is the ability to understand the causes of things.)
from Lucretius

Periclitor ergo sum. (I risk, therefore I am.)
with apologies to René Descartes

Unk-Unks
(July 2000)

Some years ago I heard the term "unk-unk." It referred, I believe, to aerospace engineers who theorized that their craft would inevitably be affected by "unknown-unknowns," events or sequences of events that simply could not be imagined by prevailing knowledge or by extrapolation of existing information. Their point: we should always be prepared for unimaginable and unexpected events. Scenario planning helps. So does lateral thinking, but most unk-unks remain beyond human estimation. Several months ago, a risk manager asked for some comments of possible solutions. There are no easy ones. Contingency planning may help prepare an organization and its people for unusual events, but flexibility, adaptability and ingenuity permit an organization to survive an unk-unk.

Part of our problem lies with our over-reliance on technology, lulled by its extraordinary track record of recent success. At the far end of any curve lie the demons of the unknown. We, as managers and advisors, must continually counsel about these remote possibilities—even beyond the one percent threshold. That means keeping something in reserve for contingencies out of simple prudence and humility.

I suggest five steps in contemplation of the inevitability of unk-unks:

1) Extrapolate from the past to the present and future, assuring yourself that you have canvassed the past as broadly and deeply as feasible.
2) Prepare scenario analyses, employing both experts and non-experts (but not necessarily astrologists or religious fundamentalists) in considering a range of alternative futures from one or more events.
3) Try some serious lateral thinking, moving deliberately away from the rational to the constructively irrational.
4) Prepare a solid contingency plan, linked to sufficient resources to meet the worst cases.
5) Acknowledge that these risk assessments and resources will inevitably be found wanting!

Autopoiesis
(September 1996)

Richard Lowther, the well-read risk manager of Brown & Williamson, in Louisville, Kentucky, sent me an email that challenged my vocabulary and view of risk management:

> I recently read *Microcosmos*, by Lynn Margulis and Dorion Sagan, and was struck by the following passage: "To be alive, an entity must be auto poietic, that is, it must actively maintain itself against the mischief of the world. Life responds to disturbance, using matter and energy to stay intact. An organism constantly changes its parts, replacing its component chemicals without ever losing its identity. This modulating, holistic phenomenon of autopoiesis, of active self-maintenance, is at the basis of all know life; all cells react to external perturbations in order to preserve key aspects of their identity within their boundaries."

> For myself, I am thinking of renaming Risk Management at Brown & Williamson the department of Autopoiesis. The only

problem I can see is that even fewer people would understand what we are about, but at least fewer people would mistakenly believe that they knew!

Lowther's quotation confirms what my wife has been telling be for thirty years: risk management is natural—an expression of common sense. Perhaps, as Margulis and Sagan believe, our species will evolve to compensate for various risks. Even so, I hope that the discipline of risk management can help speed the process, accelerating the learning curve so that we encounter fewer disasters along the way.

> *"I take risks when I must. You cannot do business without taking risks."*
>
> *"That is so. The important thing is, to be clever about* which risks.*"*
>
> **A.S. Byatt,** *The Babel Tower,*
> **Random House, New York 1996**

Paleotempestology
(April 2000)

I never thought that you could predict the future by putting your head in the sand, but that is exactly what a researcher at Louisiana State University has done. According to the *Economist* (February 26, 2000), papers at the annual meeting of the American Association for the Advancement of Science addressed our growing ability to predict major hurricanes. Forecasters are more accurate in predicting storm paths but their intensity remains difficult to determine. Given the enormous influx of people and property to the Atlantic and Gulf coastlines of the United States in the past fifty years, our better knowledge of storm paths and intensities helps officials to know when to call for evacuations. But as storm-related deaths and injuries drop, property damage erupts, in part from the failure to prohibit building on suspect terrain and to enforce realistic building codes in storm and water threatened areas.

The radical change in actual and potential damages also threatens insurance companies. We are learning, however, about the effect of thermoclines—the layers of cooler water beneath the surface—on hurricane intensities, and we now can build reliable models to assist insurance companies to determine fair rates for property owners in storm-prone areas. Firms such as EQE and Risk Management Solutions cater to major financial service companies worldwide. They search for new information on major storms, trying to determine if there is a distinct long-term pattern for these events.

A Florida State University researcher has discovered such a pattern for "big" storms, those that respond to Pareto's Law: 20% of all storms produce 85% of losses. Ocean circulation affects the position of the normal high-pressure zone that sits off the Azores and this zone in turn affects the spawning of cyclonic depressions that spin westward toward the Caribbean and the U.S. coast. Other researchers confirm an overall cycle of 20 to 40 years in which major storms range from a low of about 1.65 a year to a high of 3.5 in occurrence.

Finally, Kam Biu Liu, at Louisiana State University, has plunged a proverbial head in the sand to look for traces of old hurricanes in preceding centuries. Since the big ones surge over coastal dunes, dumping their debris into inland ponds, he dredged into these ponds and discovered that, over some 5000 years, at 22 different U.S. sites, the big ones (category four or five) occur on average about once every 300 years, with a higher frequency along the U.S. Gulf Coast. If these data are correct, and if global warming does not have a significant effect on the conditions that spawn big storms—two big "ifs"—insurance companies should be able to face future losses with greater predictability and cover the resulting losses without fear of bankruptcy. All this research has a lovely name: paleotempestology.

Variations on a Theme by Fowler
(August 2001)

Mid-summer is a time for railing at petty annoyances. I'm thoroughly annoyed by my brother's answering machine. When I call, his voice says, "we're presently out." This is, in my opinion, a gross misuse of the word "presently." He means "now" when the word means "in a short time or soon." He disagrees and, since he is a schoolteacher, I'm constrained to listen to his argument. He cites Houghton Mifflin's *American Heritage Dictionary,* Third Edition, which argues that it can be used both ways. I cite *Fowler's Modern English Usage,* Oxford University Press, which confirms that it once meant "instantly," but, after the 17th century, it came to mean "in the near future"—especially in English authors of the 18th and 19th centuries. You can't read Trollope, Austen, or even the more recent O'Brian, and use "presently" to mean "now."

Despite the overwhelming number of words in the English language, expressing every nuance of meaning, we find ambiguity at every turn. Sometimes this ambiguity can be useful. When my children used to ask me, on a long drive to Maine, "When will we get there?" I could in good conscience reply, "Presently!" They thought I meant almost immediately, versed as they were in the vernacular. What I meant was "in two or three hours," and the ambiguity kept them quiet for a spell.

What does all this have to do with risk management? We find the same ambiguity in the terms we use for predicting the future, and often this lack of clarity helps us. "Likely," "probable," and "possible" appear frequently in the risk assessment lexicon, but what do they really mean? When a CEO asks of a risk manager, "When will an 8.0 earthquake hit our Tokyo or San Francisco plants?" a response using a term of ambiguity equal to "presently" can spare us considerable difficulty. If we say the risk is one in 100 years, we are still left with the possibility that it could happen today, a century from now, or anytime in between. The ISO Working Group on Risk Management Terminology wisely refrained from attempting to define these words, allowing some essential ambiguity to remain. All this confirms the wisdom of Dr. Kenneth Arrow's affirmation in 1972 that risk "comes trailing clouds of vagueness."

I asked three of my readers for comparable terms of ambiguity in French and Japanese.

Hugh Rosenbaum, bilingual in French and English, offered a close parallel to "presently." "Incessament" meant "constantly" from the 13th to the 19th century, similar to our English word, but now it means only "right away." Another is "éventuellement." It has never meant anything other than "in case it happens," or "in case you want or need to." It never means "it's going to happen one of these days," and can lead to confusion in French loss protection instructions.

Chris Lajtha, of Schlumberger, in Paris, suggested three words for consideration:

"franchise" It can mean both "frankness" and "insurance deductible." Confusingly, the French "franchise" does not mean the same thing as an Anglo-Saxon "franchise" in the insurance context.

"vulnerabilité" It translates into both "exposure" and "weakness," giving a somewhat one-sided, negative connotation to exposure.

"prevention" It translates as "risk control" and includes both loss prevention and loss reduction. This is not confusing to the French but may be when moving from French to English.

Kazuhiro Goto, with Mitsui Marine Research Institute, in Tokyo, notes that there are four sets of symbols describing risk management and three for the general idea of "safety," this in a language short on words, where symbols may have many meanings and shades of meaning:

1. リスクマネジメント:risuku manejimento (risk management)
2. リスク管理:risuku Kanri (risk management)
3. 危険管理:kiken kanri (risk management)
4. 危機管理:kiki kanri (risk management or crisis management)
5. 保安:hoan (keeping condition safe or harmless)
6. 保全:hozen (making condition safe or harmless)
7. 防災:bousai (prevent or eliminate disaster or loss)

The ISO Working Group's document on Risk Management Terminology has been officially approved as a global guideline, providing some consensus definitions for our global discipline. Even so, ambiguity will necessarily continue, just as it has with the word "presently."

Gawsh, GARCH!
(February 2003)

As I travel through journals, articles and books written at various levels of complexity, I often stumble across a word or phrase that boggles the imagination. Being an acolyte of the E. B. White and William Strunk Jr. school of written expression—that is, simpler is better—I use these words as examples of what to avoid when we press our suit for the discipline of risk management. I found just such a phrase in a recent article by Mark Kritzman in *Economics and Portfolio Strategy* (January 15, 2003). GARCH stands for "Generalized Autoregressive Conditional Heteroskedasticity" and it is pronounced very much like the Walt Disney character Goofy pronounces "Gawsh." It is a method, as Kritzman explains, "for estimating variance from past values that does not assume variance is stationary." It is used in "maximum likelihood estimations" when "we believe that volatility evolves as a sequence of high and low clusters." I'm sure GARCH is a remarkably efficient tool for statisticians, mathematicians and almost certainly actuaries, but it is brain numbing for this humble word-spinner. Use it in a technical paper but please avoid it and its kin in materials destined for the lay reader. Or at least define it in layman's terms, as Kritzman thoughtfully did. It's too easy to astound and amaze your readers with a complex word or phrase, but the downside is obfuscation.

Another comment in the same Kritzman paper reminds me that a fresh perspective of what we do in risk management can create new understanding. The author quotes Harry Markowitz's paper, "Portfolio Selection" (*The Journal of Finance* March 1952). Markowitz divides selection into two stages, the first of which "starts with observation and experience and ends with beliefs about the future performances of available securities," while the second "starts with the relevant beliefs about future performances and ends with the choice of portfolio." Isn't this as concise a description of risk management as can be found in any of the academic journals, national standards or consultants' materials? It is brief and simple. The Markowitz sequence, modified, is:

1. Use observation and experience to create models of future outcomes.
2. Make choices based on those models. Repeat.

Compare those two simple steps to the longer and more complex approaches of the U.K. Government, the prevailing Standards in Australia,

New Zealand, Canada, Japan and United Kingdom, and the materials pumped out almost monthly by academics and consultants. Of course, there is more to "risk management," but by reducing it to its simplest parts we have a better chance to incorporate it within management culture. That's the long-term goal, to achieve a Marxist-Leninist "withering away" of the process so that it becomes part and parcel with conventional management thinking. We should not be afraid to re-state what it is that we do more simply.

Risk Management Clichés Strike Again
(June 2003)

Earlier this spring I chanced on my old friend, C. Lee Shay, hiding warily behind a telephone pole. As I had not seen him in some time, I asked where he'd been.

Shay: Unfortunately I was doing time, sent up the river to the Big House, to the slammer, by the Language Police for impersonating an officer. They assumed that I was a CEO, CFO or CRO by my language. A clear case of mistaken identity!

Editor: How can that be?

Shay: Well, I was embroiled in an enterprise risk management project. I found a champion who was ready to enact a robust program, embedding a value-added concept that would empower the troops from the get-go. We designed the matrices, stimulated networking, touched base with senior management and started bottom-up and top-down analyses.

Editor: Did you use consultants?

Shay: Certainly. They swarmed like ants over our organization and created a ten-pound report recommending a set of deliverables that would resonate with all our stakeholders.

Editor: What happened then?

Shay: My go-to guy did it! It was do-able and he got buy-in! He rolled out the value proposition and ramped up our core competencies. He was da man!

Editor: How did he do it?

Shay: He created a set of proactive enablers and sent them cascading through the company.

Editor: And all this was a win-win situation?

Shay: Absolutely! As we drilled down into the organization, we achieved alignment, and created competitive advantage.

Editor: Didn't any of this put them to sleep?

Shay: Not at all! We prioritized our steps, utilized our skills, incentivized the troops and maximized our margins. All our Zs were stacked in the same direction!

Editor: But why are you still hiding?

Shay: Those language cops are still after me!

Editor: What do they want?

Shay: Closure, you fool, closure!

With acknowledgement and apologies to Roger Angell, of The New Yorker, whose Chip Arbuthnot is the model for this dialogue.

> *The good days are gone. What fools we were. We were in cliché heaven, and then, almost overnight—just think about it. "Slippery slope" has bottomed out. "Arguably" is worth pennies today. "With all the bells and whistles" is a dead guppy. "No-brainer," "my plate is full," "written in stone," "it isn't rocket science"—these were blue chips just last year. All gone-zo. My portfolio is tapped.*
>
> **Roger Angell, "The Cliché Expert in Recovery,"**
> ***The New Yorker, February 17 & 24, 2003***

CHAPTER 13

Postscript

Now we come to endings.

One of my favorite authors, Patrick O'Brian, had a persuasive view, voiced through his character, Dr. Stephen Maturin, in *The Nutmeg of Consolation*:

> "There is another Frenchman whose name escapes me but who is even more to the point: La bêtise c'est de vouloir conclure. The conventional ending, with virtue rewarded and loose ends tied up is often sadly chilling; and its platitude and falsity tend to infect what has gone before, however excellent. Many books would be far better without their last chapter: or at least with no more than a brief, cool, unemotional statement of the outcome."

Billy Vaughn Koen had an even better idea. The end of his *Discussion of the Method* is entitled "An Anachronistic Preface" in which he suggests that the reader start anew at the beginning, armed with all that has been learned, so that the second reading begins real enlightenment!

Over the years, I've been intrigued with the postscripts and sighoffs used by various writers and radio-television dignitaries. I was weaned on Jimmy Durante's "Goodnight, Mrs. Calabash," and the classic final rejoinder of Bob Elliot and Ray Goulding: "Write if you get work and hang by your thumbs." More recently Kurt Vonnegut used "and so it goes" in his novels, a resignation to a world apparently out of control. National Public Radio's *Cartalk* ends with the two brothers, both roaring with laughter, advising listeners in turn, "Don't listen to my brother!"

And, again for those who have access to radio in North America, there is Garrison Keillor's famous signature advice at the end of each week's *Prairie Home Companion*—"Be well, do good work, and keep in touch."

I'm content to use my own postscript, one that I use for my children, three of whom are or have been teachers: "Teach important things." It's a reminder that we are all teachers in risk management and that we need to recall each day what is important in what we do.

> . . . life is best lived 'with one eye cocked toward Comedy and the other eye skewed toward Tragedy,' and that 'out of this feat of balanced observation emerges Humour, not as a foolish amusement or an escape from reality, but as a breadth of perception.'
>
> **Judith Skelton Grant, quoting Robertson Davies, in** *Robertson Davies: Man of Myth,* **Viking, New York 1994**